A SPECIAL NEED FOR MUSIC

By Jim Howell

To Tom, Nancy, and Danny Holliday: without you,
I never would have realized that there was a special need for music.

To Jim, Marcia, and Carson Shamel: without you,
I never would have tried to fill the special need for music.

With much love, thank you!

Jim Howell

TABLE OF CONTENTS

PART 1: PROGRAM OVERVIEW

WHEN THE STUDENTS ARE WITH ME,
THEY GET TO BE ROCK STARS!

In 2009, I created a hand drum group for students with special needs. At its peak, we had a class that met regularly for about fifty minutes once a week at both the middle and high schools. We hosted at least one performance each school year. During our time together, we've been featured in the newspaper, in a documentary film, and even on a famous rock band's website. In 2020, I started a music program for adults with special needs. The age doesn't matter; the meaningful performance at the end of our sessions can be life-changing.

Our hand drum groups provide a performance experience to part of the student population that usually isn't offered such opportunities. Now they have a chance to showcase their abilities. For many of my students, the hand drum group has become the highlight of their education.

Not only is it educational for the students, but it's fantastic for their families, too. Parents and loved ones can see their children succeed with others. I've had several parents tell me how great it was to watch their child perform a concert as a member of a group in front of an audience. Everyone loves applause and cheers!

The program also has several academic advantages: it can reinforce studies in math, support speech development, enhance motor skills, and improve coordination. But most importantly, it gives them an identity.

This program is not a modified lesson or a watered-down version of a band or choir class. This is a performance ensemble created specifically for students with special needs so they can experience a group performance like other students.

I hope this book will provide tools to help you fill the *"Special Need for Music"* in your life.

ALL YOU NEED IS AN OPEN MIND

It's not important to be a music educator to have success teaching drumming to students with special needs; you don't even need a musical background! We don't use written notes or sheet music in our studies. All teachers need is an open mind because everyone can share music.

I've worked with many different adult assistants in my groups: middle school and high school teachers as well as classroom aides and paraprofessionals. All of them were able to function well in our group. Not one of them was a drummer or university-trained musician.

When it comes to playing musical instruments, there are a million different ways to learn and everyone thinks their way is the best. But no matter who your teachers are, which methods you study, or what materials you buy, there's only one end goal and that is PERFORMANCE.

So often when we say the word "performance" we think of rock stars playing for thousands of screaming fans in gigantic arenas, or pop stars performing their latest hits on TV in front of millions of viewers. But sometimes we forget performances can be small, too. Musical expression comes in as many different forms as it does people performing it. That's what makes it so important.

Whether you're playing for a crowd of 10,000 people in a stadium or for Grandma and your stuffed animals in your bedroom, you are performing. You are actively creating art for someone other than yourself. You are feeling emotions in your music and communicating them to your audience. It's like giving the audience an emotional hug or saying, "Look what I can do!" without speaking a word. For those of us who are unable to give real hugs or say anything to our audience, being part of a performance provides an experience much more meaningful than others may ever know.

My goal for the readers of this book is to gain enough confidence to incorporate music into their learning environment, whether as an educator or an advocate for success. I hope my method of sharing music helps unlock some hidden talents. Hopefully, your excitement will inspire people to achieve success in ways they never had access to before, or maybe never even considered.

WHAT IS SUCCESS IN MUSIC FOR STUDENTS WITH SPECIAL NEEDS?

Success is different for everyone. Maybe for one student, the idea of just hitting the drum might be a great accomplishment. There might be another individual who can already keep a steady beat and perform complicated rhythms, but now they can perform in a group with other students for their parents. We must consider what success looks like for all of our students and respect that it might not be the same for everyone.

I believe anyone can enjoy, learn, and perform music. For music teachers, all you need to do is revise your definition of success. For special education teachers, all you need to do is learn a couple of beats. No matter what your background, this book will allow you to find success for everyone and help fill the "Special Need for Music."

THE TARGET AUDIENCE

I started working with students with special needs when I was teaching seventh and eighth grade; later, the program was extended to include sixth-grade students. After developing a class at the middle school over a couple of years, I was assigned an additional position at the high school. I adapted the whole concept to that age level, too. The transition was easy because I already knew most of the students. We were able to revisit some of our favorite tunes and we learned some new stuff, too.

My hand drum groups were always an extra activity that the special education teachers and I would support. It was never an assigned class. We tried to keep the format as consistent as possible, but sometimes changes in the schedule made meeting more difficult. Sometimes we had to get creative and take what we could get, even if it wasn't a weekly class.

Most recently, I was approached by the owner of a vocational program for adults with disabilities who wanted to bring music to her organization. She developed the idea from a newspaper article featuring one of my presentations. It turned out she had three of my former students in her program, so now I have adult students who were part of the original group. Over time, it became clear that age doesn't matter.

The target audience is whoever needs it!

A NOTE TO THE MUSIC PEOPLE

This program certainly isn't the traditional "follow-the-conductor" ensemble. When I started working with students with special needs, I had to let go of my music teacher background a bit and approach the task not as a hand drum specialist, and not as a music specialist, but as a teacher in the most basic form. I needed to rethink what I thought was the "proper" rehearsal technique, playing position, posture, stroke, sticking, and (the most difficult for me) tolerating a less-than-steady beat.

When I started my hand drum classes, the students had no concept of what we were about to do. Every time I start new students, the beginning is far from drummers playing drums. But as time passes, I am continually surprised by how much improvement each student makes. Since I was the only band director in the district, I usually had students from sixth grade until they graduated. I could see the development of the students over time. I also learned more about their personalities and could develop better ways to help them as individuals. In the adult groups that I've worked with it's the same; over time, there's always some type of progress no matter the age or abilities of the students.

As the years passed, I had students who could easily be part of my marching percussion section. I have also had students who never could keep time. But that's not the point! There are all kinds of growth, development, and learning. Progress is different for each individual. For students who can't communicate or don't typically show any emotion, performing at a concert and showing excitement and joy on their faces is huge progress. Even if students don't play a note, a parent seeing their child have pride with a group can be the greatest form of progress of all.

Music teachers might need to unlearn what they know and sacrifice some of the things that matter in the "traditional" performance ensembles to make this work. Once you free your mind, you'll have one of the most rewarding musical experiences of your career.

HOW IT STARTED

One day, a teacher at my former junior high school approached me about one of her students. I didn't know her that well, but I knew that she worked in what used to be called the MH Room, which stood for Multiply Handicapped. I had never worked with any of the special education teachers before. I had no experience with students with special needs and no training except a class called "Special Education Law" that I took as a part of my graduate studies.

The course had nothing to do with teaching actual kids, but it opened my mind to how complicated and ever-changing the requirements of special education really are. It also taught me an appreciation for how special education has changed over the years and continues to evolve.

The teacher explained that a parent had contacted her and wanted her child to be in the band. She said the boy couldn't speak, had low signs of sight, and didn't have much ability to hold anything. This sure didn't seem like someone who would do well in the band. I couldn't understand why the parent would want to put her child in a position where he would surely fail.

As it turned out, the mother was trying to communicate with the teacher that the child seemed to respond well to music, and the parents wanted him to be around music. She wondered if he could sit in on

Carson Shamel was my very first student. He is pictured here with one of his fantastic aides, Jackie Clarke.

practice sometime during the week. I didn't know this until *years* later. When I began working with the student, I was under the impression that I needed to figure out how to have this boy with special needs play in the band.

Sometimes people who don't have a background in music think band directors just pass out sheet music, give the students instruments, and quickly put together songs that sound like a recording. The public often has no idea that there are specific skills that need to be learned for each instrument and that the ability to read and perform music in a group needs to develop over time. I'm imagining the parent's point of view; she probably doesn't know a lot about music and thinks band class is like listening to the radio. She wants something positive for her child, and she's considering anything and everything that might give him a good experience at school. I'm thinking she's not realizing any of the mechanics that go into young band rehearsals. But I can't blame her for trying; I would do the same if he were my child.

To start, I suggested meeting with the student during study hall once a week to play conga drums. I didn't have a class at that time, so there wouldn't be other students in the room. There would be no interruptions and he would have my full attention.

For our first meeting, we each took a drum (including his teacher so she could help him). We tried playing together. I played beats and he rocked back and forth. Occasionally he would touch his drum. For the most part, his experience seemed positive, so we continued with weekly lessons. At one point, the teacher brought the student with an aide and I gave the aide a drum too. It worked! The aide learned right along with us.

One day they came into the room while I was listening to a CD. He began bouncing up and down while entering the room, making vocal sounds and movements I had not seen before. From then on, we started using recorded music as a part of our lessons. I would play a CD on the big classroom stereo and play along on my drum, encouraging him to do the same. He responded well. There were times that he would not just touch his drum but actually hit it.

Later in the school year, I suggested she bring all the students with special needs to our lessons. I'll never forget the look on her face!

PART 2: SKILLS AND CONCEPTS

Carrie Carpenter and Ryan Murphy encourage each other during a performance.

THE VALUE OF MUSIC EDUCATION

Many schools offer music education based on the idea that learning an instrument helps students excel in their academic courses. While this may be true, most musicians will tell you that studying music is important for its own sake, and that actually performing music is more helpful to students than simply taking a course. The performance element develops an emotional connection. When students perform, they are actively creating art. Unfortunately, performance is most often left out of the overall music education experience for students with special needs.

We will cover basic techniques and musical concepts as we go, but remember that extensive musical study is not required by teachers or students to have success. As long as there is an interest in sharing music, there is a place for everyone at some level. If you're new to the music scene, you might end up seeking out more information and that's cool too!

Sometimes we encounter people in education that don't understand the intrinsic value of music education as we do. They want us to make connections to other subjects to justify "playing" music during school time rather than making it an extra-curricular activity. If you find yourself in a position where you need to advocate for music education, there are a variety of additional skills and concepts that music performance reinforces. Below are some of the many non-music concepts and skills that show up in our sessions.

> The word "play" is used to describe what we do with musical instruments as well as what children do with toys. Sometimes I think that can mislead people who are not musicians. To help avoid that association, say "performing music" instead of playing songs or "performing on instruments" instead of playing instruments.

Following Directions

In the beginning, students learn basic techniques to get started. We start with very simple instructions and add more steps as we go. As time progresses, we add more movements, rhythms, and songs, increasing the complexity of instructions.

The Group Dynamic

Working on music in this program requires individuals to work together as a group. There are many opportunities for students to learn to work together and interact with each other. Performances can involve even more social behavior than just the weekly class. When getting ready for a performance, the preparations can turn into a unit entirely separate from the music.

Coordination and Motor Skills

There are many physical elements to performing. Students learn how to move their hands and arms in specific ways when learning to drum. They learn to sit a certain way and demonstrate good posture in each session. We also add movements to songs that reflect lyrical content or musical elements. When using smaller instruments, students learn where their fingers go, how to grip the instruments, and how to control them to get the proper sounds.

Fractions

The concept of one thing being half of another can be reinforced when teaching music. The idea of *two being half of four* and the idea of *doubling four to get eight* comes up from time to time in our playing. Music always relates to math.

Comparing and Contrasting

Many musical terms can be presented as a comparison. Consider the concepts of loud and soft. You can't have just loud or just soft; it has to be soft compared to loud. For example, soft means a low volume, but how do we know what low is? It's softer *than* what? Loud means a high volume, but how loud should it be? It's louder *than* what? Soft and low are similar and loud and high are similar. Explaining the similarities and differences between the two is a great topic for discussion and could certainly be related to many lessons outside of music.

Music and Speech

We often use speech to learn rhythms. Identifying syllables and copying the natural rhythm of words to play beats can help kids with pronunciation. For example, in one of our weekly activities, students use their name and something they like in a sentence and associate it with a rhythm. "Mikey likes pizza" is a great example. This can also build confidence to speak in front of others, especially when students lead the exercise.

Leadership

Students have opportunities to lead different activities or parts of the class. Leadership builds self-confidence, which promotes positive interactions with others through communication.

Communication

Students need to communicate when they perform, both with teachers and other students. For non-verbal students, playing music can be an alternative method of communication or an outlet for emotion. There's also room for the inclusion of students from other classes, gifted programs, and student leadership or peer mentoring programs.

Spelling and Vocabulary

Often students are required to study spelling and vocabulary in their academic subjects. I include a list of terms at the end of each section that can be used for this purpose. Sometimes the lyrics of the songs we use can introduce new words to students, too.

The Concert

There are so many different aspects of a concert that can be educational. Not only can each student learn from preparing the music for the actual performance, but they can learn from planning the event, too. The preparations for a concert can teach valuable life skills. Sometimes as listeners or audience members we take for granted the behind-the-scenes work needed to make a great show. Students can learn to develop pride in the steps that need to be taken leading up to the event.

Teachers can reach out to community members and promote their programs outside of school, building positive public relations. Families can celebrate together, building self-confidence that continues long after the performance has ended. Best of all, the complexity of the concert can be as complicated or as simple as needed. A small concert in a classroom for parents during the school day can be just as impactful as a performance in a large-capacity auditorium.

Putting It Together

These concepts are all related and can usually be found in each of our sessions or classes. If you need to justify your lessons to your supervisors, you can relate any of these topics to content standards or learning goals. You can also collaborate with teachers of other subjects as you explore the non-musical elements needed in a performance.

As you learn more about these ideas throughout this book, you will be able to relate them to your own teaching environment and create truly meaningful educational experiences for your students.

PART 3: EQUIPMENT

DRUMS

I'm a firm believer in the concept of anything is better than nothing. When I first started, I had a couple of old congas and djembes. The mixed instruments were not ideal, but it was all we had. For my students, it was outstanding. They had never played a drum before, so anything they were able to play was awesome in their eyes. They didn't care about colors, quality, age, how worn the head was, and if the drum was out of tune with itself or even un-tunable. We also used an old stereo from the 80s. It was big, but it was not made for a bunch of drummers to play along. It didn't matter. Nothing mattered except the experience of playing a drum like we were rock stars!

Drumhead

Djembe

Conga

As the class evolved, it became clear that having a group of kids playing drums was extremely worthwhile. Luckily, there was time available in the master schedule to allow for a weekly class. The transition to a regularly scheduled class required some adjustments to our sessions.

One thing we learned is that when choosing equipment, it's always okay to make accommodations to include somebody. It's much better to use an instrument that can be played easily than to give a student an instrument that might not suit his or her situation to make the group look the same. It's important when working with students with special needs to put the individual's needs ahead of stage optics. Sometimes what makes an instrument the worst choice for one student might end up being the best choice for another. With that being said, I have tried a whole mess of different instruments over the years, and I can offer some insight as to what worked for my students. Basically, we needed two things: instruments and a sound system.

There are a gazillion different hand drums on the market. Drum companies seem to be creating new instruments all the time. For me, the conga drum is the best choice. (Many people mistakenly refer to conga drums as bongos. Keep in mind that bongo drums are the smaller pair of drums that the player usually plays between the knees while seated.)

You can see the difference between bongos and congas in this photo. Bongos are the little ones, and the conga is the big one.

The conga drum is an instrument that is used in many pop, jazz, and rock groups and is almost always found in school band programs. It's available from most reputable music stores. The height works well for middle and high school students to play while seated, and it sounds good when placed flat on the floor.

All the major drum companies offer a budget-priced student conga drum that is perfect for our class. At 28 inches high, these drums are slightly shorter than professional drums. This makes it easier to play while seated. The playing surface, which is called the head and produces the sound, is also important to consider. The diameter of a conga head is usually somewhere between ten and thirteen inches. If you're using different-sized drums, sometimes the students having more difficulties will do better with the larger playing surface. The more experienced players and staff members can use the smaller surface. Student-line congas typically come in a set of two with a stand. I don't use the stand with my students; we always play seated. But storing the stands always gives you the option in the future.

Quality Counts

Even though we're choosing student line instruments, it's important to get a quality brand of drums made to be played by musicians. These are the kind you buy at a music store. Avoid tourist souvenirs or drums designed for decorations. Name-brand drums will last longer, sound better, and replacement heads and parts will be readily available.

We had a situation in the early days where the head broke on a generic drum. The company that made the drum was no longer in business. I tried to get a replacement head, but the only one I could find was another brand that didn't quite fit.

Heads

Most conga drums come with skin heads. The skin heads provide a sound that blends well when in a group. Synthetic or plastic heads are usually louder and can "stick out" if you have a mix of skin and synthetic heads in your group. If one student is using a plastic head and the others are using skin heads, his or her sound will be louder than the rest, and the other players will tend to follow the loudest drumming instead of the song. The great benefit of using synthetic heads is they are not affected as much by the weather as natural skins. The drum companies are making synthetic heads that seem to get better all the time and they're quickly gaining popularity, but at the time of this writing, I'm not yet using them in any of my groups.

STANDS

There are two different kinds of stands. One is a double stand that holds two drums and the other is a basket-style stand that only holds one drum. Basket stands usually allow more flexibility in positions, allowing the user to position the drum at a variety of angles.

Basket Stands   **Double Stand**

The double stand often requires both drums to be mounted to function properly. Some double stands go higher than the basket stands.

Both stands are designed for players to use while standing, and as I mentioned earlier, we always play seated. In some of my larger groups, I sometimes stand to teach and use a basket stand for my conga so I can be seen better. In a smaller group, I don't use a stand to teach; I usually just sit in the front of the room in a chair facing the students with my drum on the floor.

AFRICAN DRUMS

Many teachers ask me about African drums, particularly djembes. I tried djembe drums and they didn't work well for our situation. When placed flat on the floor, they sound muted and they're too short, placing the body in an uncomfortable position.

Jason Fickes, drummer at Advocates for Success from New Philadelphia, Ohio, shows us the height difference between a conga and a djembe. Djembe drums are often shorter than congas and can be difficult to play for most people when placed flat on the floor. However, they can sometimes be perfect for someone in a wheelchair when placed on a stand.

If you're using real African imported drums, tuning, finding replacement heads, or repairing this very specialized instrument can be quite difficult. I took lessons from a drummer from Ghana and learned how to work with and even make the heads, and it's not easy. I've also received authentic African drums that arrived with authentic African bugs in them! I had to find a specialist who could remove the bugs. So, for our purposes, the real African drums were not a good choice.

Although not a good choice for the group, using a djembe did help me solve a problem. I had a student in a wheelchair who only had the use of one hand. She couldn't reach a conga on the floor, and putting one on a stand made it too high above the wheelchair. We were able to mount a small djembe on an angled drum stand. We made a nice name tag and it looked just like the others. Using a djembe ended up being a great solution for a student who couldn't reach the conga.

Maintenance

The drums themselves don't require much maintenance, but it's important to take care of skin heads. When the weather gets dry, when it's super cold in the winter and heaters are running, the heads will tighten and you may have to loosen them with a tuning wrench. When it gets humid, you may need to tighten them. As we said before, synthetic heads don't have this issue when it comes to humidity.

It's a good idea to use hand lotion while playing. It's good for the skin heads, which are often dry (especially when they are new), and tends to smooth out any imperfections. It also protects the players' hands and helps the heads feel more comfortable.

When drums are new, they're almost always shipped with low tension and the heads will usually need to be tightened. Whether skin or synthetic head, the drum will need some type of adjustment. All new drums come with a tuning wrench. Synthetic heads aren't affected too much by humidity like the skin heads are, but all drumheads are affected by repeated use and will loosen over time even if they're tuned really well.

When most people hear the word "tuning", they often think of the strings on a guitar. The player adjusts each string until it produces an exact note. When tuned properly, the guitar will sound correct when the player strums all the strings. Each string works together to make the sound of the guitar.

Drums can be tuned too, but we aren't looking for a specific note or pitch like other instruments. Most people refer to tightening the head or loosening the head, rather than using musical terms like "sharp" or "flat." When we tighten heads, we are raising the pitch, and when we loosen heads, we are lowering the pitch. On each drum, there are tuning bolts often called tension rods or lugs. Each one has a nut that can be turned to adjust the tension of the head. You want each nut to be the same tension. Just like guitar strings, the tightness needs to work together. For the most part, the drums will sound best when they are at a medium tension. Naturally, the smaller drums will have a higher pitch and the larger drums will have a lower pitch.

Keep in mind, the drums will still work even if they aren't in perfect tune with each other. A professional drummer will be picky about tuning, but we aren't looking for perfection. There are many videos online about tuning conga drums. It's really not difficult at all. You could also ask a band director or contact a music store or professional drummer in your area if you have trouble.

In the end, the process has to work for you. We are not professional congueros, we are educators, so don't worry about perfection. Do your best and have fun!

HAND PERCUSSION

In addition to drums, hand percussion instruments can be a great addition to your ensemble. Two common hand percussion instruments are maracas and tambourines.

If you decide to add maracas, it's important to buy quality instruments to avoid replacing them frequently.

These maracas have a contoured handle that can help students with their grip.

I use the larger plastic ones with a wooden handle. They are a bit louder and sometimes slightly more expensive than the cheap wooden "touristy" kind, but they last forever. The larger handles make it easier for students to hold them. If you have someone with limited use of their hands or fingers, there are smaller options available. Teaching students to hold and play the maracas properly can help with the dexterity of fingers, hands, and wrists.

Tambourines are also great hand percussion instruments. I have found the best tambourines are the budget-priced models with a synthetic head and a single row of jingles. I have tried the tambourines with a double row of jingles. They were too loud and too expensive. The fewer jingles, the better for our situation as it will keep the volume at a lower level.

I recommend a tambourine with a head so the players can strike it with their hands. You can shake a headless one and strike it on your palms, but a head is better for individuals with reduced motor skills. It gives the players more of a target to hit and creates more sounds. I've tried the wood shell tambourines with real skin heads and double-row jingles, but after a humidity change, we had a lot of trouble with the heads becoming too tight or too loose. Many of the nails came out and we were losing jingles constantly. I didn't want someone to get hit with pieces that were coming off, so I re-glued the nails. I spent way too much time trying to fix them. Plus, with the wood shells, one drop can break the whole instrument. In the long run, they weren't worth the hassle.

One nice thing about the tambourine is almost all of them have a hole in the shell to mount the instrument on a stand. Students will often think it's for their fingers, but it is actually there to attach to some type of hardware. If you have a student who has limited ability to hold items, you can use a cymbal stand. Cymbal stands are very adjustable and can help you position the instrument however you need.

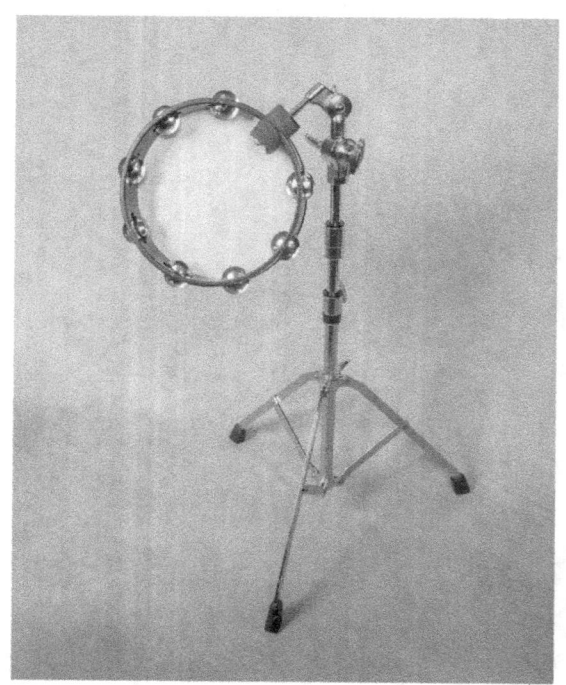 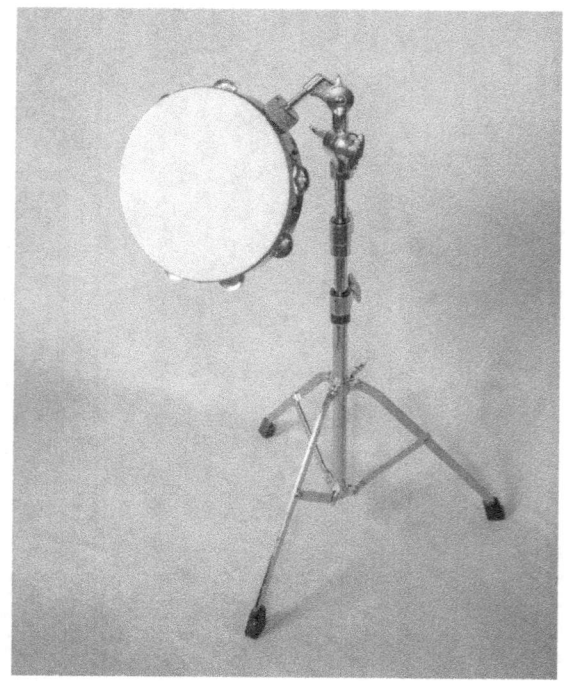

AUDIO

When performing with recordings, a PA system or very large stereo is a must. If you try to use computer speakers, a boom box, or a small wireless Bluetooth speaker, the students will have a difficult time hearing the music over the drums. Large speakers and a lot of wattage from an amplifier can make it simple for music to be set at an appropriate volume.

There are many small PA systems sold at music stores that are portable, affordable, and easy to use. It's the kind of setup a DJ would use at a wedding or dance. So often, teachers are intimidated by an audio setup or PA (public address) system, but there really isn't much to it. There are four things in any audio setup: speakers, amplifier, mixer, and cables. That's all you need. Just make sure you can connect your sound source to it. You can go old-school and use a CD player or use your phone as your sound source. Many modern sound systems are combining the amplifier and mixer into what is called a powered mixer. Some companies are making speakers that are powered, too. As long as you know what you have, it's pretty easy to make it work.

Remember, all these components (mixers, amplifiers, speakers, and cables) need to be the kind of products that are made for musical performance or commercial use. You should purchase the equipment at a music store or an online site that specializes in performance equipment. Avoid home electronics or big box stores. I started with a large home stereo in the beginning, which was fine for three people, but once we started a class the system just couldn't produce enough sound for everyone to hear.

Always be sure your speakers and amplifiers will work together before you buy them. Be sure to ask someone for help. If they are sold as a package, they are usually paired to work together, so that is the easiest option. Most often, the smaller, affordable packages come with passive speakers and a powered mixer, which is a combination of a mixer and an amplifier. Powered mixers are perfect for a smaller setting. I recently discovered a speaker that was powered, had inputs that replaced the mixer, and featured Bluetooth, a true all-in-one device. I have yet to use one, but they are becoming more popular and worth consideration. I will talk more about sound systems when we discuss playing with recorded music.

PART 4: GETTING STARTED

LOGISTICS

Keep in mind many of the pictures in this book came from my largest groups. I've also had small groups with only three students and three staff members. I started the program with just one kid and his teacher. Size doesn't matter. Providing a musical experience to someone that otherwise wouldn't have one is what matters. Whether you go all-in and buy drums, tambourines, maracas, and a sound system that would make any rock star proud, or you only use a couple of maracas, you're still making a difference. Let's consider some of the elements that will make it easier for us to begin making music with students.

STORAGE

The first step is to plan where the class will meet and where the instruments will be stored when not in use. All the school groups I've had over the years have met with me for drum class in a room that's not their regular classroom, but that doesn't have to be the case. Some creative use of space can work wonders. My groups usually met only once a week, so the instruments were in storage more than they were played.

While maracas and tambourines don't require much space, drums are large and can take up a lot of classroom real estate. Also, it's nearly impossible for a student to walk by a drum without touching it. Prepare a way to handle the students who are not using the drums. This becomes more important when using a shared space. Always try to keep the drums out of sight and out of reach when they're not being used.

One way to save space is to stack drums head-to-head. When stacking them head to head, you have to be careful not to damage the heads or accidentally knock one over. When it's time to use the drums, I get them down, and then the students can handle them. When we put them away, I am the one that stacks them. This method of storage should only be used if the teacher is stacking the drums.

In this picture, the drums were being stored in a room with other percussion instruments. There were times when another music teacher used the room for small groups when I wasn't there, but for the most part, the drums were not bothered. The way the drums were stored doesn't allow wandering fingers to find a place to visit.

The nice thing about hand drums is they are quite sturdy. They can literally take a beating! Accidents happen, so don't be too upset when one of your students sits down and puts their feet around the bottom of the drum and knocks it over. That's when I learned how important it was to teach students how to sit. The drum goes between the knees and both feet should be flat on the floor.

Chance Iannone safely carries a drum by the rim.

When you expect kids to carry the drums they must be taught how to do so safely. They need to use two hands and lift the drum using the rim. This was something I learned the first day when one of my drums got "up close and personal" with the tile floor! This is a great reason to always have more drums than you do people just in case you have a problem.

While replacement parts are usually available for name-brand drums, they will often take some time to deliver. Most music stores don't stock conga drum parts; they have to be ordered. That's why having a backup drum (or two) is a great idea.

When you're writing a grant, always ask for a little more than you need. You might unexpectedly gain a student. We had a student move into the district mid-year and because I had an extra drum, we were able to include everyone without missing a beat (ha-ha, pun intended)!

If you don't have an extra drum for a new student, he or she could always use a drum used by a classroom aide or teacher to fill a sudden need. I've played on broken drums and tambourines a couple of times. It's usually not a problem for the staff, but it can make a huge difference for your students. It's important for the students to always have working instruments.

STARTING SOMETHING NEW

My students reminded me very quickly it's a big deal to do anything new. We all know this is true, and we have all experienced it. Whether it is leaving for college, moving to a new city, finding a new home, beginning a new job, or getting married, all of us have experienced the stress that comes with change. I'm not sure why, but for some reason, I wasn't thinking this way when I started my drum groups.

I thought that when the kids came to my room for the first time, I would tell them to have a seat, distribute the drums, and the kids would begin playing. That's not what happened.

It took a long time to start. Our first meetings were basically just learning a routine. I was learning just as much as the kids. Over the last several years, I have developed the *top five things my students taught me* about logistics.

1. Have the exact number of needed chairs set up before the students enter and each child needs to have an assigned seat. There can be no music stands, extra chairs, or instruments in the way. This sounds simple but it's easily overlooked. Even with the classroom aides and the teacher present, the process of telling the kids to move the music stands and sit in the front row did not work.

2. Students should line up at the door and wait for me to lead them in. This will only take seconds, but it will save several minutes each session, and it will keep students from getting confused and frustrated. Sometimes the kids were coming from different places and arrived at different times, which could cause disruption and confusion when trying to get seated. When they waited at the door, I could put them in a specific order to assign them seats. I could also find out if anyone was missing then remove a chair from the setup if someone was absent. After I had the right number of chairs and the kids were in the right order, we "follow the leader." I was the leader, and they followed me to their chair. I walked in front of a curved row of chairs and showed each person where to sit. The aides and teachers had a place to sit, too, usually next to a student that might have needed extra guidance After everyone was seated, we received our drums. The aides and teachers got drums, too. Once the kids had the hang of things, usually after a few classes, a student could be the leader.

3. Students need to be given a drum. It cannot be up to them to choose. When there are a variety of drums in a room and you instruct a student to get one, it can be very confusing. When I first tried this, I didn't realize some of the students had never even seen a drum before. I found out later that some felt intimidated because there were so many to choose from, how would they know which one to choose? So instead of taking a drum and sitting down, they just stood there looking sad and anxious. Sometimes they would argue about who got the red one, and then feelings were hurt. We hadn't even started, and we already had tears!

> If you're buying new drums, it's a good idea to get drums that are all the same color. It gets frustrating when students are upset because they "wanted the blue one this time!"

To make things run more smoothly, I started putting the drums out before the students came in the room, and then I would put them away when we were done. After the students progressed, I started having them put the drums away. Then at the high school, I could have the students set up the drums at the beginning of class and then put them away at the end.

I have certain drums that I give to certain students. The stronger players get the high-pitched or smaller drums. This typically includes staff members, but remember just because a person is a staff member doesn't mean they can keep a beat. I find the high-pitched drums project more and the other players can latch on to the sound. The low-pitched drums can be more forgiving and hide inaccuracy easier than the high-pitched drums. The larger drums are also easier to play with both hands. Any students who may have trouble getting both hands to work together should use the larger drums.

4. Students need to be seated first. After they're seated they can get their drums. This is especially important in the first meetings. Giving students their instruments one at a time may be the best way to keep order and reduce distraction. It's important to have a way to keep your drummers from playing before being instructed to do so. I had a great teacher that always called it "noodling" when students were playing when they weren't supposed to. When I was first getting started, I had them put their hands on their heads if they were able. This prevented noodling. As students get older, I don't need to do it as much. For the most part, my students don't play when they're not supposed to. If they do, I put my hands on my head and they do the same.

In this picture, I had the chairs set up in an arc in front of some large speakers and the drums in a cluster away from the chairs. This way I could lead students to their chairs, then give them a drum.

5. If things aren't working, maybe I need to change. This was the most important lesson I learned. It sounds silly, but I had to remember this whole concept was new, so there were no rules or any structure other than what was typical in my band classes. It was becoming clear that this situation was totally different! I had to be even more flexible and open-minded than usual. What works for some students might not be a good fit for others. As educators, we all know this, and we adjust accordingly. I continue to learn every time I meet with students.

LABELS & NAME TAGS

Once seats are assigned and the arrangement is working, I create name tags for the seats. This way the students can learn how to come into the room and find their places on their own. They are to pick up their name tag, sit in their seat, and hold it until I collect them. I keep them in order so it's easy to set them out at the beginning of the next class.

I like name tags. I use them in all of my band classes as well. They help me learn names, they make it easier to assign seats, and once they are on the chairs, I can easily put specific drums in front of specific individuals before we start. I use a piece of copy paper folded in half and write on it with a big marker. I make one for each kid and adult that sits in the chairs. Sometimes the classroom teacher or aide can help make them, or if you are lucky enough to have student helpers, this is a great task for them.

At first, it might be helpful to attach the nametag to the drum, but after I get to know the students, I usually just use them as a tool to show each person where to sit. When it comes time for a performance, they usually make big, colorful tags that can be part of a larger project. It could even incorporate the art teacher. If that's not feasible, students can always work with their teachers and classroom aides to make great name tags. Be sure everyone understands that they need to be easy to read from a distance. When the drums are set up for a performance, having a large name tag on the drum can also help the audience know where their family member will be so they can choose their seat appropriately. I like to encourage my groups to make name tags that are better than mine. They always rise to the challenge!

STUDENT HELPERS

Having student helpers makes life easier for the teacher, but it's also a great educational experience for the students. Learning how to interact with students with special needs is important at any age level. Years ago, at my former high school, a couple of the band students had a study hall during the same period as the drum group. One day they asked if I needed any help setting up, and ever since then, student leaders have been a big part of what I do.

Sometimes they set up chairs, but sometimes I need them to move our concert band setup to accommodate the drummers. Usually moving music stands and positioning chairs is a great help. Having my band students set up the drums saves me a ton of time.

Some schools have honors groups, student leadership programs, or mentoring programs that are perfect for this. All you need to do is talk to the adult leader of whatever group you want to include and you can find out what the group's strengths are. Sometimes they have a project that requires certain elements that can be found in our program. All you have to do is ask.

One year, a group of students was in charge of decorating before the concert. As part of another class, they worked together to make a specific design relevant to their project and our performance material. They covered the instrument lockers with artwork and interesting facts about our songs and styles of music.

SEATING

There is almost always a need to sit a certain way. I like to have teachers and classroom aides spread throughout the group. Staff members in the group can help a student who needs extra attention. Teachers and aides who can keep a steady beat will certainly help those students who are having trouble. Students seem to musically "follow" the staff.

Once the seats are assigned and everyone is in the right place, have the students practice taking the correct seat by following an assigned leader. Ask the students to stand, then follow the leader out of the room into the hallway and stop. The leader on the way out will end up being the last person in line when the students come back in. The leader coming into the room sits in the furthest chair and the rest fill in. It's a good idea to practice coming in and out a couple of times. This exercise is also useful in a performance situation when the students need to "take the stage" in front of an audience. Most of my school groups didn't make a formal entrance at our performances because I didn't want to cause extra anxiety. It all depends on your performance area and the needs of your students.

SAFETY

In recent times, it has become very important to assign instruments as well as seats for health reasons. Sharing instruments or other classroom materials can sometimes be a bad idea. Putting a label on a drum is easy. Sometimes you can attach a name tag to the drum and store it with the name tag attached. You can also use mailing labels or tape to put names on drums. Just make sure the label is something that can easily be removed. Painter's tape, Scotch tape, or other clear office-type tape comes off easily…packaging tape does not!

Smaller hand percussion instruments like maracas could also be labeled and/or cleaned before they're put away. It all depends on your situation. You can make a game of it and put all of the used instruments in a bin or basket and call it the "dirty laundry." After cleaning, the instruments will return to wherever the "clean laundry" is stored. Some of my students ask if they can collect the dirty laundry. I bet their parents wished they did that at home!

FUNDING

Money can be hard to come by as budgets are being cut more and more. The great thing about my drum group is that all the equipment is relatively cheap compared to other instruments and other educational materials. At the time of this writing, you can usually find a conga drum for less than $300, a tambourine for about $30, and maracas for about $30.

My former high school drum program was entirely funded by grants, except for the speakers and sound system. The school already owned them. Some schools have portable PA systems that many people aren't using, or at least not frequently. I have found old PA systems in storage closets in auditoriums and gyms at more than one school. They were old and dirty but they worked!

As a new teacher, writing a grant was intimidating. But after the initial experience of figuring out how to meet the criteria, I realized that there really isn't much to it, you just need to complete the paperwork. Usually the more money you're requesting, the more writing you need to do. Try to be creative where you can be, and offer pictures when possible.

When applying for different grants, remember you won't get them all. Don't take it personally, your proposal just didn't fit into their financial plan. Plus, you don't know who else applied and what the decision-makers were looking for. Just because you don't get your first proposal doesn't mean you will never get it. Keep trying. Your students are worth it. Keep in mind that many school districts can offer professional development credit towards license renewal for time spent writing grants.

I've found many times that if you have no money, there's usually someone who will give you some for a good cause. Sometimes all you need to do is ask. Local businesses sometimes budget money specifically to give away. There are historical foundations and fraternal organizations like your local Eagles Club that will sometimes donate, too. Don't forget about alumni foundations. They sometimes have money specifically to give to education.

Fundraisers are always an option, too. In all my years as a teacher (I started teaching in 1998), I've seen students sell everything from candy bars and pepperoni rolls to bed sheets and laundry detergent. I even know a school that had a gun raffle. It was their most profitable fundraiser ever!

PART 5: INSTRUCTION

TECHNIQUE

I like to think of technique in layers. Depending on the needs and abilities of the students, the technique can be different. The first layer is the most basic. If we can develop further, that's great, but there is nothing wrong with participating in the most basic way possible. What's most important is the awesome opportunity to play a drum for the first time. It's not just being a listener, but an actual performer!

Professional musicians are a great source for learning technique, but they are usually teaching students to be future professionals. That's not what I'm looking to do in my classes. My philosophy of teaching technique is to do it simply and efficiently. I want to get the most amount of people involved and do it in the shortest amount of time possible. That gives us more time to play our instruments!

While most professionals think there is a right way and a wrong way when learning to play the congas and other percussion instruments, for our purposes it is important to make things work for everyone. We want to include all students no matter what and everything can be modified. Sometimes trying to learn the proper technique helps some students develop new skills, but playing "correctly" can sometimes discourage others.

I always leave it up to the classroom teacher, aides, or paraprofessionals to determine that balance. Let's face it, we all know our own students. Dexterity and fine motor control can be strengthened by playing drums and percussion instruments, but progress can be hindered by hurt feelings and frustration. By presenting technique in layers, you can easily incorporate everyone.

Let's take a look at the parts of the drum first so we know what we're playing!

NOMENCLATURE

I've always loved that word! It means the names of parts of something. It's a much cooler way to say "parts of the drum!" As I mentioned earlier, the drums we use are called conga drums.

PARTS OF THE CONGA DRUM

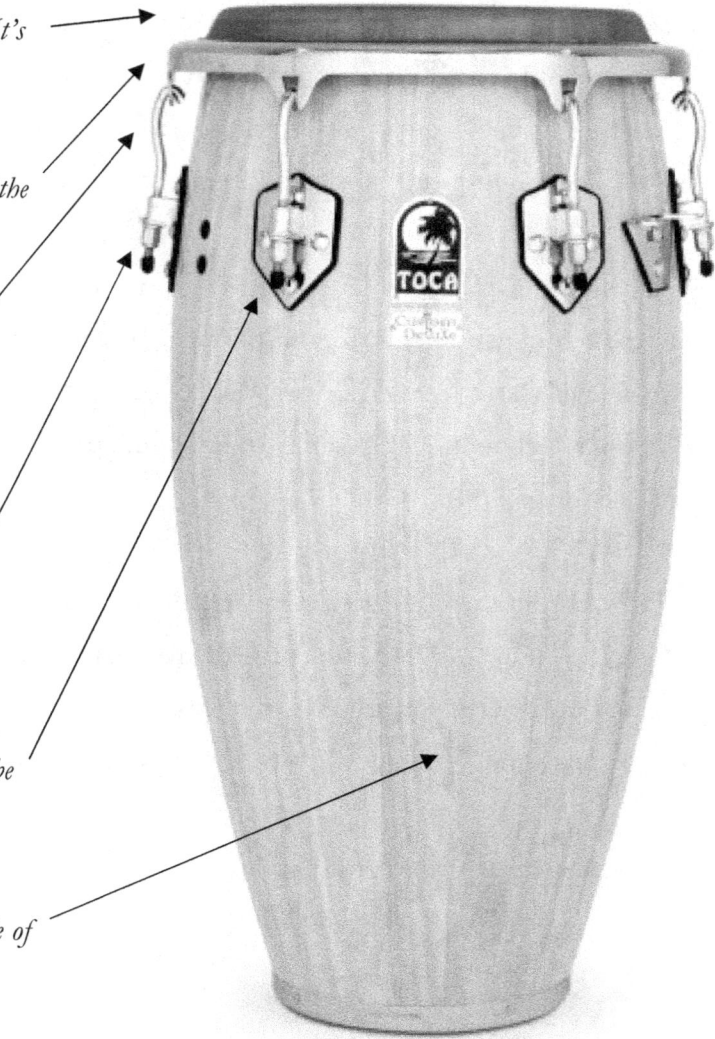

Head: The part at the top that we strike. It's made of animal hide or plastic.

Rim: The metal ring around the outside of the head. It holds the head to the drum.

Tuning bolts: These are the hardware parts on the drum that hold the head in place. They are sometimes called tension rods or lugs.

Nuts: These are the parts you turn to adjust the tension on the head.

Side plates: They allow the tuning bolts to be attached to the drum.

Shell: The large tube part of the drum made of wood or fiberglass.

POSTURE

To help with proper posture, it's important to use standard open chairs, not the kind with arms or desks attached. The students should sit on the edge of the chair and place the drum shell between the knees, not too close or too far. The distance is correct when the student can comfortably place his or her hands on the head in a playing position. When the drum is between the knees, there is no need to wrap the legs or feet around the drum; they should rest comfortably at the sides of the shell. I always have my students keep the drum flat on the floor. Most professional conga players tilt the drum when seated, which will always sound louder, but that's not what we're after. A lower volume is best, and it's much safer for students to keep the drum flat on the floor.

This position can of course be modified for those who are unable to sit in this way. It's more important to include someone than to have them play in the "correct" playing position. For extreme situations, there are drum stands that might help position a drum for a student who otherwise can't reach it.

55

PREPARATION

I always have a bottle of hand lotion available when students are playing hand drums. I squirt a few drops on each skin drumhead. Rubbing the lotion into the head will keep the head nice as well as help the hands. Playing hand drums often seems to dry out hands, especially in the winter. Dry skin can crack, and it can be painful. I keep the lotion handy in case anyone needs it. New skin drumheads are often very dry, especially the inexpensive ones, so this practice helps maintain the heads as well as make the players more comfortable. If you get to a point where your drums seem slimy, you've probably used enough!

HAND POSITION

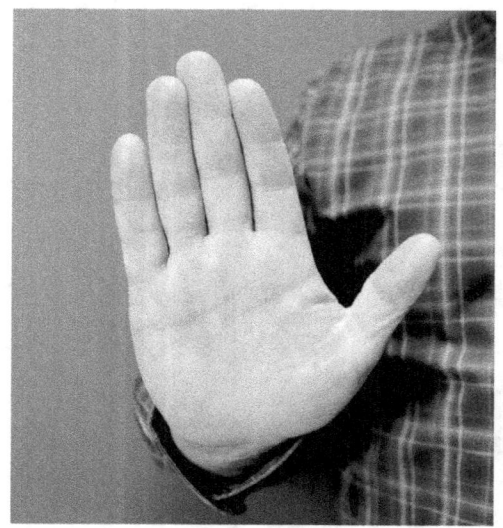

When we begin, I put my hand up vertically with my fingers together and my thumb out. I always say, "Fingers together, thumb out of the way."

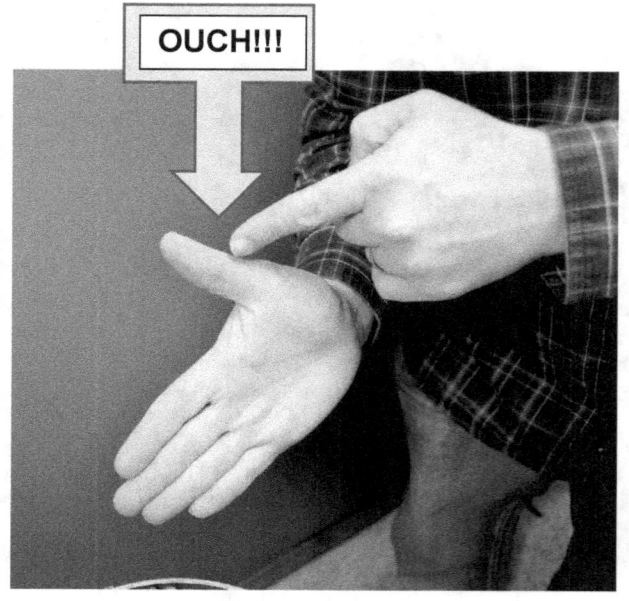

OUCH!!!

Be very mindful of the thumb. It really hurts when you smack it against the rim! It happens to everyone at some point, but we need to avoid it as much as possible.

Now we need to think of a triangle from head to elbows. Also, a triangle from elbows to hands.

Some of our students may not have the ability to have their bodies in this way, so I avoid saying "proper playing position." We can modify this posture for our students. For example, one year I had a student who had trouble using one of her hands. We made the best of it and didn't make her feel like she was failing if she only used one hand. Some days she could get both hands working together, other days not so much. If you have an occupational therapist at your organization, this can be a great topic of future conversation for them. If you're like me and don't have that type of resource, just do your best to make the student feel included.

One of the things I like to say when things don't work out for someone is, "We all have different strengths." It's the same with both kids and adults. Some stuff we just don't get, but others do. I'm terrible with directions, but my wife knows exactly where we are all the time. I can get lost in my own neighborhood, and she can tell you which way is north like she has a compass in her nose. BUT, if I ask her to roll up an extension cord or a garden hose, I might as well be asking her to put six angry cats in a pillowcase with one hand covered in Vaseline! The students need to know they may find success quickly when learning a technique, but other times it might take a while.

STROKES

Strike the drum with a relaxed, light, and easy stroke. The drum will only play so loud, so if you hit harder, it will just hurt your hands; it won't get louder. I tell kids to use an "easy stroke" or to "play lightly." I've had some drummers get too excited and play too hard, but volume isn't about hitting hard. To play loudly, we need to think of our hands moving higher, and to play softly our hands move lower. I try to remind them that we can have fun and be excited and still play lightly.

For the most part, we use two strokes: the open tone and the bass tone.

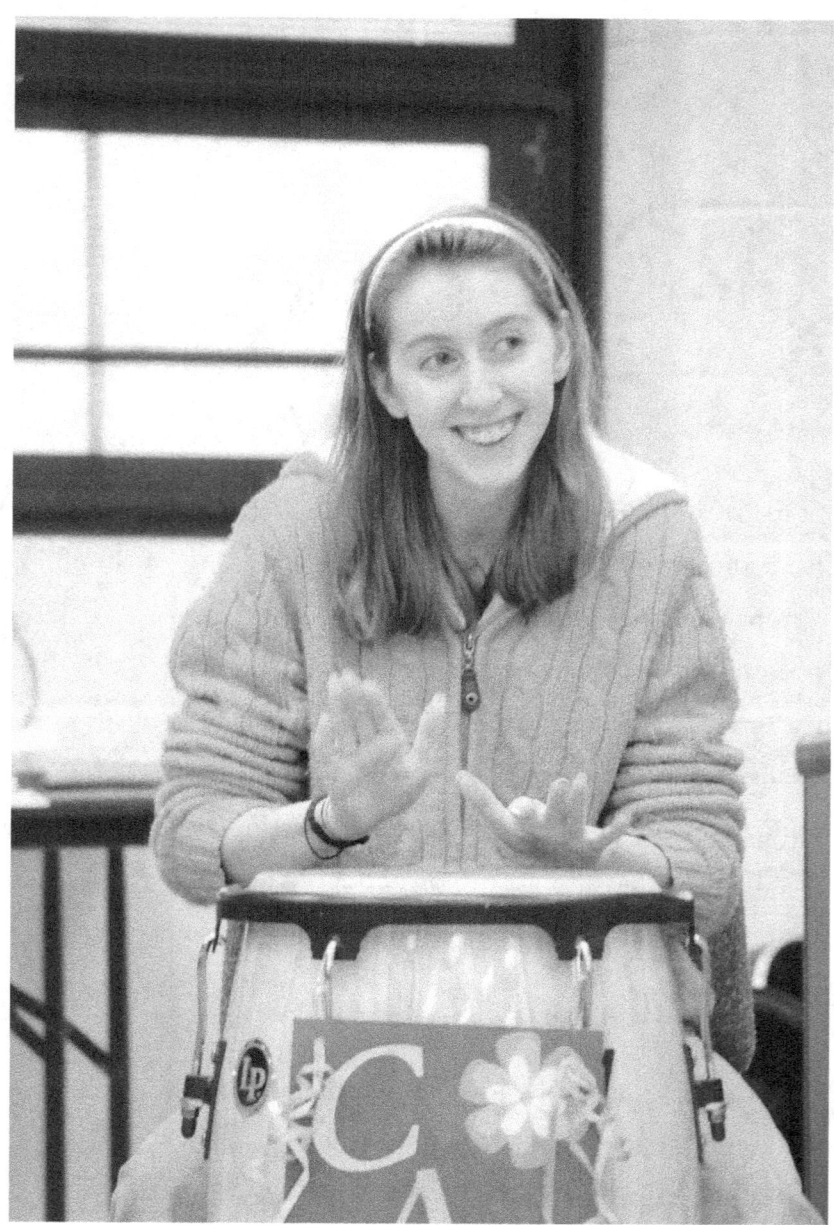

Carrie Carpenter demonstrates open tones during class.

OPEN TONE

For the open tone, the fingers should be together and strike the edge of the drum. It's important to use mostly fingers on the head to avoid bruising the part of the hand where the fingers meet the hand. The fingers need to be together as much as possible to make the full sound. If you strike the drum with your fingers apart, the sound is thin.

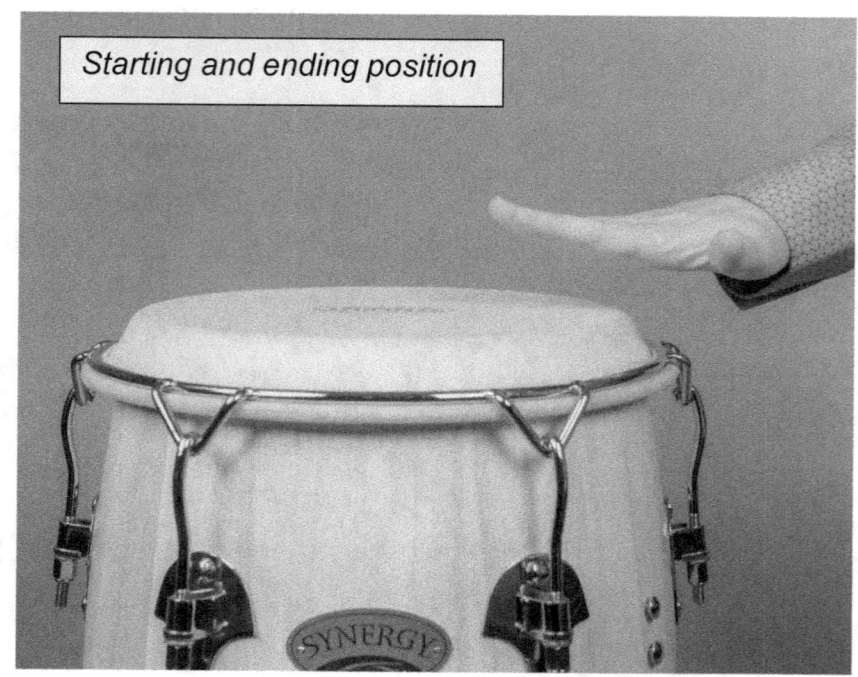

Starting and ending position

It's important to let the drum head vibrate. We need to get our fingers off of the head right away after we strike the drum to hear the tone. I always tell my students to think of the drum as if it's really hot. If you touch a hot stove or frying pan, you move quickly to get your fingers off because it will burn your skin!

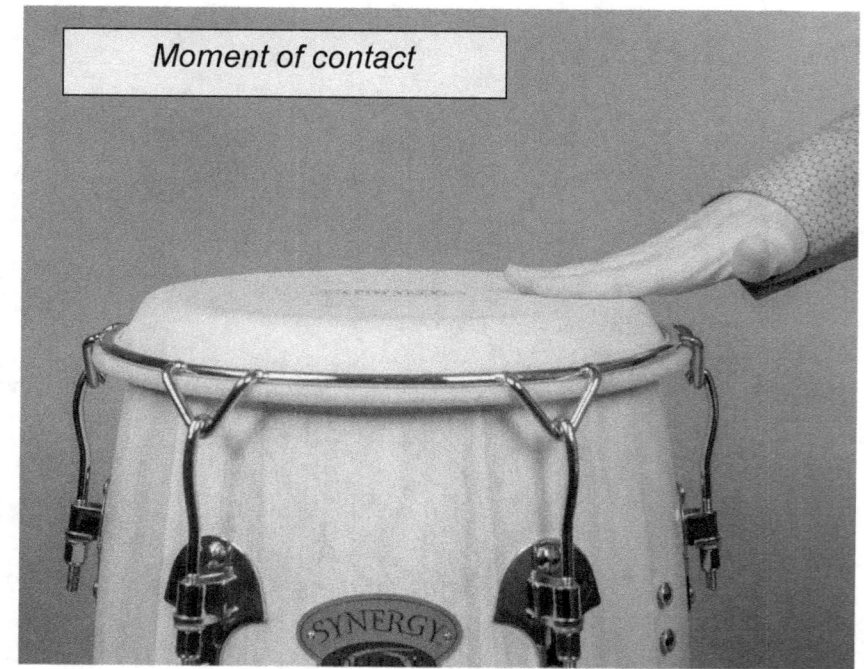

Moment of contact

BASS TONE

For the bass tone, we strike the drum with the palm right in the center. The fingers aren't important in this stroke, the sound comes from the palm.

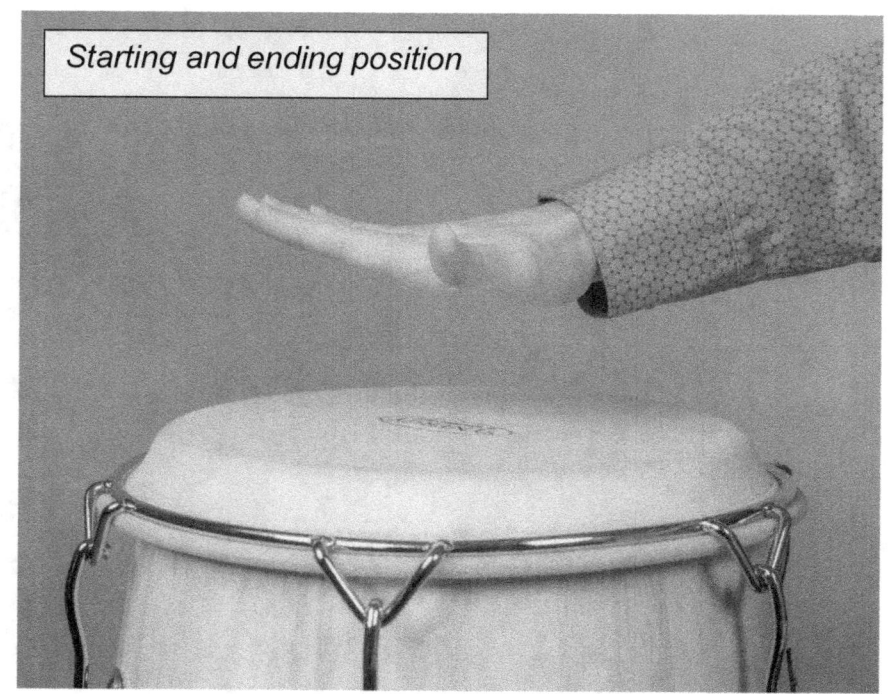

Starting and ending position

It's a much more muted sound than the open tone, especially when the drum is on the floor. Remember, for our purposes, leaving the drum flat on the floor is the best choice.

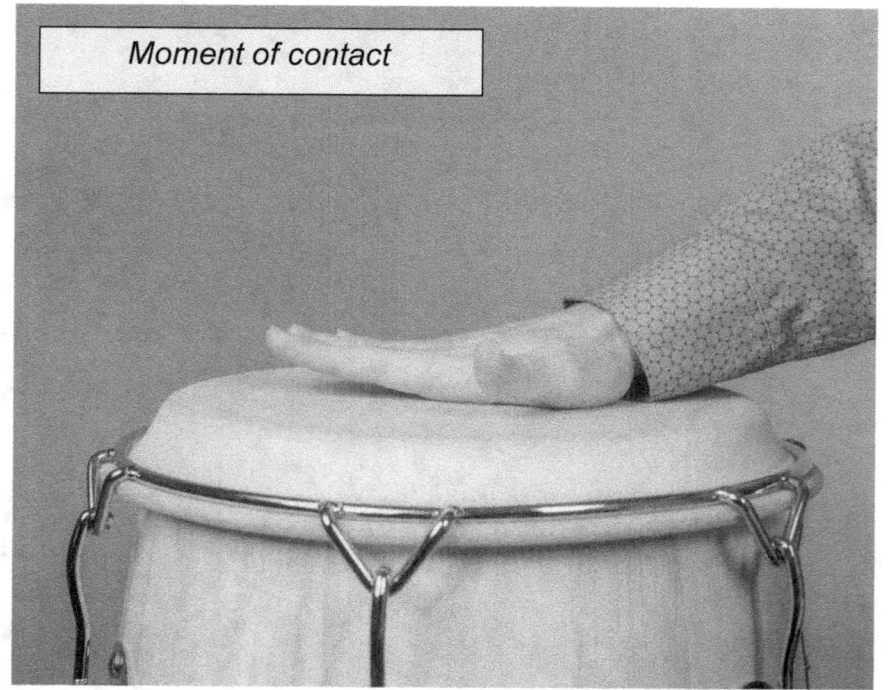

Moment of contact

UNDERSTANDING DIFFERENT STROKES

If students are leaving their hands on the drum, pushing into the head, or holding their hand against the head, let them know they're creating a closed tone, and that's a different technique than the open tone.

I demonstrate by holding my hand on the drum, pushing into the head, and telling them it's closed. Then I encourage the movements for the open tone by demonstrating the hand coming off quickly, allowing the sound to come out. Although the closed tone is not a stroke we use, sometimes teaching it can help students understand how the open tone is played. The contrast becomes key. With the open tone, we need to think of pulling the sound out of the drum, whereas the closed tone pushes the sound into the drum.

Sometimes studying hand position can help students understand the difference between the open and the bass tones. If students understand that the bass tone is in the center and the open tone is at the edge, there should be less confusion.

When teaching this way, you're not just demonstrating the strokes, you're teaching the concept of contrast, open vs. closed stroke, fingers off vs. fingers on, short sound vs. long sound. These relationships can be incorporated with other classroom lessons for all students.

Vocabulary words that were used in this section:

CONCEPTS	DRUM PARTS	BODY PARTS
Ouch!	Conga	Hand
Posture	Drum	Fingers
Stroke	Shell	Thumb
Open Tone	Head	Palm
Bass Tone	Rim	Knees

RHYTHM

I don't talk about rhythm at first. I just work on helping the students to make a sound. After the sounds are starting to make sense, I start to teach the open tone with a steady beat.

I start with eight beats using each hand separately. As we play, I count out loud with them, "One, two, three, four, five, six, seven, eight." Then I say "switch" after the last beat and we switch hands and continue the exercise with the other hand. Sometimes if needed, the instruction "switch" will replace the "eight" and sound like, "One, two, three, four, five, six, seven, switch." Remember the word "seven" has two syllables, so don't accidentally add an extra beat. After a few times with the open tone, we practice with the bass tone.

Next, we practice a combination of four open tones, then four bass tones with one hand. As we play, I now say each stroke instead of counting. As we play the strokes, I say, "open, open, open, open, bass, bass, bass, bass." Then we switch. I say the word "switch" in-between beat "eight" and beat "one" of the next exercises. If doing so creates confusion, just like before, the word "switch" can replace the eighth beat in the exercise. It would sound like, "open, open, open, open, bass, bass, bass, switch" and then we use the other hand.

Sometimes, as students become more comfortable with the techniques, they want to speed up, so we need to make sure to use a steady beat. All these exercises can be practiced at different speeds. Sometimes learning to play rhythms both fast and slow can help students better understand the difference between the two. That difference can be applied to or related to other lessons outside of music.

This is the time when we learn the word "alternate." I always say that alternate is a word that means to go back and forth. I like to use the example of how people naturally alternate their feet when they walk. Now we learn to do these same exercises with alternating hands. We play eight open tones, "Right, left, right, left, right, left, right, left." We practice this a couple of times, then try the same with the bass, then open and bass tone combinations. Although we start with using eight-beat groupings, all exercises can be done in groups of four as well.

There are many drummers and band directors who use these kinds of warm-ups and call them "Eight on a Hand", "Eights", "Fours", or something similar. You can call them whatever you like. Essentially, they are exercises to practice strokes in rhythm. In the beginning, we work on them quite a bit.

Sometimes I can move to individual students and play with them a few times while the group is playing to help them with their hand positions. As time moves on, the amount of class time for these exercises lessens, but we still always run through them. In the first class, we could spend five to ten minutes learning the strokes and fifteen minutes with the exercises, but after we've had four or five classes, we might only spend five minutes with the strokes and exercises in total.

THE ROLL

Usually, students are quick to figure out when they play really fast it sounds cool! Playing fast is called a roll. Whether you teach it or not, everyone's going to try a roll, so we might as well start with it, especially when one of the students does it first.

When you play a roll, you alternate your hands and move as fast as you can. The lower you keep your hands, the faster you can go. Plus, it will produce a softer sound. To get louder, move your hands higher. When I use the roll with my students, we don't worry about keeping a beat.

My students always love to do "the wave" in our groups. We see the wave in the audience at sporting events and concerts. We also see it on stage in dance routines. It's a simple movement, like putting your hands in the air immediately after someone else. Dancers might do it in a line where each person drops to one knee right after another. When drumming, it's great to do "the wave" with the roll.

Just like an audience member in a stadium puts their hands up following the person next to them, a drummer can strike the drum after the person next to them. Each person starts his or her roll softly, plays louder when the wave gets to them, then goes back to playing softly when the wave moves on. I like to lead the wave by pointing my finger at the students as we go around the group. When the finger comes to them they get louder, and when the finger moves to the next person, they go back to playing softly.

Another fun thing to do with the roll is a stop-and-go game. Start with everyone quiet and ready to play. You say "GO!" and everyone rolls for a bit, then yell "STOP" and everyone stops. You can repeat this several times and it can be quite fun. I usually start with open tones, then after a few times, I'll use bass tones. If you have trouble stopping the exercise, you can put your hands on your head and lead them to do the same. It's a great way to help students follow the teacher, all while practicing the strokes. In a typical music class, we might call this "following the conductor".

Vocabulary words used in this section:

CONCEPTS	TECHNIQUES	COMMANDS
Switch	Alternate	Stop
Eight	Roll	Go
Four	The Wave	

PAT AND CLAP

If you start playing with recorded music, you may discover that you need a little more variety than just keeping a beat on a drum. You'll find as you start working that patting your legs and clapping your hands is a great way to add variety or change up a verse or chorus of a tune.

Patting

When seated, patting the legs is simple. The hands are held with the palms facing down to hit the legs. Both hands are moving in the same direction at the same time.

Clapping

When first teaching my students, I realized not everyone knew how to clap. Clapping can be a complex task because you are moving your hands in two different directions. If you've never really thought about it before, clap your hands and see which way each hand moves. For the most part, everyone claps with their dominant hand. For example, right-handed people will usually put their right hand on top. To understand this better, try clapping backwards, as in the reverse of what feels natural. It might seem strange, but it's important to feel what's happening so you can understand how to teach clapping if needed. We can always gain an appreciation for the learning process by doing things backwards. Basically, all you need to show the students is that one hand strikes the other. The dominant hand moves down

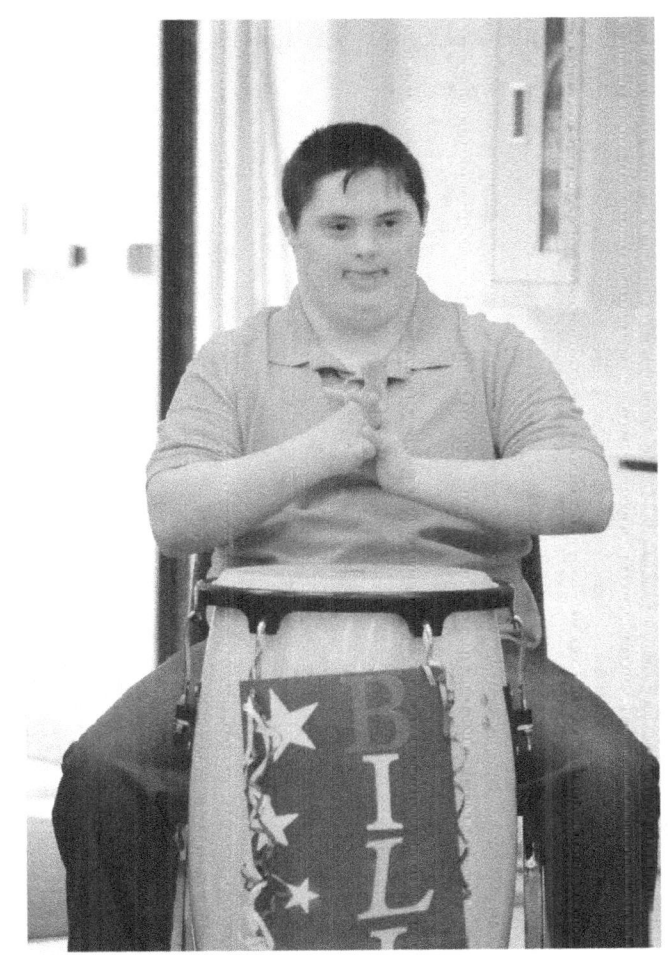

Billy Nalley demonstrates clapping during class.

while the weak hand moves up. The fingers from the dominant hand hit the palm of the weak hand. We use this concept later when we learn how to play the tambourine.

Remember to keep instructions simple and demonstrate the strokes, don't try to explain it too much. Sometimes actions are easier to understand than spoken communication.

Resting

In music, when we don't play, it's called a rest. Many times, musicians will refer to "not playing" as "playing a rest." It's important to understand that just because one instrument or person is not playing on a beat, that doesn't mean it's not there, or that someone else isn't playing. Sometimes we have to mark beats we don't play. Some music teachers might say

"Rest" or whisper "Shhh" when they don't play. It usually doesn't take long for students to figure out clapping and patting patterns so any kind of counting or vocalizations usually won't be needed once students learn the songs.

Application

Let's consider how to put clapping and patting with recorded music. For starters, you can pat on each beat for a verse, then try clapping on each beat for the chorus or next section of a song. The chorus of a song is the part that everyone knows. It usually happens a couple of times throughout the song and is always the same. The verse has different words, or lyrics, every time. Patting and clapping are simple techniques that are quick to learn and add variety to our songs. As time passes and skills progress, you can make patterns with combinations. For example, PAT, PAT, CLAP, REST can go along with a song like "We Will Rock You" by Queen.

For the most part, I use patting and clapping when there isn't much happening musically in a song, such as in an introduction. A good example is a song like "Don't Stop Believin'" by Journey. The beginning is a great place to pat for a while, then clap for a while. When the main part of the song starts, you start playing the drum.

When playing with recorded music, places in the songs where all instruments are playing are often the best place for drumming. On a song like "Stayin' Alive" by the Bee Gees, there's a steady beat with a full sound that's perfect for only drumming. When there are few instruments, softer music, or clapping and singing, I have my students pat or clap.

Vocabulary words used in this section:

CONCEPTS	BODY PARTS	MUSIC TERMS
Pat	Palms	Rest
Clap	Legs	Verse
Rest	Hands	Chorus
		Lyrics

I PLAY, YOU PLAY

"Call and response" is a great part of what I do in each class with my students. In music, this is where the leader says something and the group says something back. The phrases can be different, like when the leader says, "Shave and a haircut" and the group replies, "Two bits." The phrases can be the same, which is what we most often use. We copy each other. We "say and play." Students must say words and play the drum at the same time. We begin with one type of stroke on the drum with simple word combinations. As students develop, different strokes and more complicated rhythmic combinations can be used.

This exercise not only helps with rhythm but can promote speech development. Kids can learn about syllables and how to pronounce parts of words and put sounds together. If your students need spelling words, you can use the words presented in your exercise.

I've found it's usually hard to describe a steady beat. It's best to just model it and not try to explain it unless absolutely necessary.

I like beginning with something each student likes, maybe a favorite food or snack. Kids are always ready to tell you their favorite treat! I start by telling them my favorite food is pizza. Then I say it as I play open tones:

I   LIKE   PIZZA

If you need to, you can relate the rhythm to the students by describing it as long, long, short, long, like this:

I   LIKE   PI-ZZA
Long   Long   Short-Long

I say and play the example several times, then I ask them to copy me. I point at myself, and I play first. Then, I point at them while they play. I use pointing as a cue of when to start. I always try to stay in rhythm even if they don't.

Me:	**I**	**LIKE**	**PI-ZZA**		Class:	**I**	**LIKE**	**PI-ZZA**
	Long	*Long*	*Short-Long*			*Long*	*Long*	*Short-Long*

Even though we're not playing a song, keeping a steady beat is helpful to me and it seems to be more comfortable for everyone involved, including the staff members. It might not seem like it at first, but eventually the steady beat will help the students, too. At first, there may be no signs of a beat. It might be a hot mess! Don't worry about it; just keep trying. Maintaining a steady beat in everything we do helps develop the concept, even if it's not discussed.

Now that everyone has figured out that I really, really, really like pizza, it's time to start with the students. I ask the first kid what she likes to eat. After she tells me "cake," I say her name and what she likes as I play open tones on the drum.

CHRISTY   LIKES   CAKE

You can relate the rhythm to the students by describing it as short, short, long, long.

CHRIS-TY	**LIKES**	**CAKE**
Short-Short	*Long*	*Long*

After I say and play the "Christy Likes Cake" example, I have the kids join in. I tell them "I play" while pointing to myself, then "you play" while pointing to them.

Me:	**CHRIS-TY**	**LIKES**	**CAKE**		Class:	**CHRIS-TY**	**LIKES**	**CAKE**
	Short-Short	*Long*	*Long*			*Short-Short*	*Long*	*Long*

This can be repeated many times. Each time we practice it, I continue to stress to the students that they should try to "say and play." Sometimes we put our hands on our jaw to feel the different syllables of the words while we speak. This helps them feel how the beats line up with the words.

We can also break it down into smaller sections to help those that may have trouble at first. For example:

"Chris-ty" is two short strokes. We play that a couple of times by itself.

"Chris-ty likes" is two short strokes and one long stroke. We do that a couple of times.

"Chris-ty likes cake" is two short strokes and two long strokes. Now we've got it!

If you're wanting to reinforce speech development, be sure to do these exercises while keeping the hand on the jaw to show each syllable. When you're describing it, use the word "syllable" instead of stroke. Although I'm not a speech teacher and I don't work with one, I still talk about syllables when I use this exercise.

Be sure you have enough time to get to everyone. The students always get excited when it's their turn. If you don't get to everyone the first day, be sure to get the rest of the students the next time you have class. In a way, it becomes part of their identity and can be a source of pride as well as great fun. I make a seating chart and under each name, I write their favorite thing. It really helps me learn their names.

After everyone can tell you what they like, you can add some bass tones to the exercise. In the example "Christy likes cake" you can make "cake" a bass tone. The same with "Mikey likes pizza." You play the student's name and the word "likes" as open tones and play the food as bass tones.

As the students advance, sometimes the kids will be able to say the example instead of the teacher. It means a lot more when they do it themselves. I make it a goal for each of my experienced students to lead our group by saying their names and foods. They have to say their name, not just "I." For example, when it's Lexi's turn, she has to say, "Lexi likes tacos" not "I like tacos." Some names are more rhythmically challenging than others, especially when you get to the adults and add "Mr." or "Miss" to the name. "Mrs. Jameson likes strawberry milk" is a complicated rhythm and quite the mouthful! You could simplify that one by making it, "Mrs. J. likes milk."

I've also used favorite colors, favorite restaurants, favorite games, and favorite music. Depending on the group, sometimes I can change our topic every semester. Getting them to tell me about the music they're listening to can help me pick the music for our class. It can be helpful to choose artists that the kids like when you are looking for songs to play. It's important to explore and find what works for you. The fact that you are sitting in a room with kids and teaching them to play on a drum is already awesome!

This lesson can be used to teach the concept of *improvisation* found in many music content standards or courses of study. The students are using tools they have learned to create their own music without preparation. It's also a great example of *call and response*, which is a concept that turns up in a variety of music education materials. Call and response can be related to many popular songs from today, classics from the past, and even traced back to its African roots.

Some vocabulary words that were used in this section:

CONCEPTS	SPELLING WORDS
Syllables Call and Response Improvisation	Can be anything students like in your "I Play, You Play" exercise.

PLAYING WITH RECORDED MUSIC

After working on fundamentals and understanding some basic rhythms and stroke combinations, you might be ready to try playing along with recordings. It's not something that has to happen, but it's fun and has a lot to offer, particularly if you want to have a performance. I've found that even if keeping a steady beat with recordings doesn't happen quickly for everyone, it always improves as time progresses, especially when you have staff members participating with the students. Choosing appropriate music for your students is important because not everything works. Tempo changes, complicated beats, and a large number of independent parts can be confusing. Music with straight, simple beats and catchy melodies will give students quick success and they'll want to play the tunes again and again.

As mentioned in the equipment section, having a sensible sound system is important when playing with recordings. The music has to be loud enough to be heard over the drums. The number of people and the size of your room will determine what you need. Big speakers are a must when you have a bunch of drummers. Professional PA systems used by rock bands and DJs will give the best results. If you don't have a PA system, you can still work with a large stereo if you are only playing with a few people in your classroom. I used a large stereo every session with my middle school group, but then as we got closer to

PA stands for "public address" and many musicians will refer to their sound systems as PA systems. This way, they don't imply a home audio system. A home audio system is something you might use to listen to music or connect to your TV. We need equipment for musicians. Some music stores have these products listed in categories such as "live sound" or "pro audio." No matter what you call it, the speakers and amplifiers we need are the kinds you buy at a store that specializes in musical instruments.

performance time, we borrowed a small PA for more volume when there was an audience. All of our performances used a PA system, so when we were in a large room with more people we could still hear the music without having to hurt anyone's ears. When there's an audience, even a small one, you will always need more volume than you expect. A wide-open room with concrete walls will reflect sound. Curtains and carpeting will control the sound, absorbing some of the sound waves and keeping them from bouncing around and echoing like they do in open spaces with flat surfaces. The same is true with people. The more bodies in the room, the less echo. What seemed loud before might not be when the room fills up.

Subwoofers, sometimes just called "subs," are large speakers that only handle the lowest frequencies. They're designed to enhance the bass sound in music. They have to be used in addition to regular speakers to produce the full range of sound and cannot be used alone.

I've found that subwoofers can be very effective for students who have little ability to communicate. The vibrations can be very soothing, and feeling the beat makes everyone play better. Plus, by having a lot of bass, the overall volume can be lower and more comfortable. I had a student who was non-verbal but really seemed to enjoy songs with a lot of bass, so I wrote a grant and added some subwoofers to the system.

Most high school band and choir rooms have some type of sound system. There are large speakers in almost all auditoriums and gymnasiums. Sometimes there's a portable setup. Most schools have some sort of PA system somewhere, but if you can't locate one at your school, reach out to other teachers, schools, churches, or social gathering places, because you never know who might want to get rid of some old-school audio gear. If you need to buy one, music stores always offer packages that will have everything you need and more. My first system had a powered mixer with a set of 15-inch speakers.

After you have an audio setup that seems like it might work, it's time to try it with the students. The first step is to keep a steady beat with the music. When I first started, all we did was play open tones along with different songs. We did this with many tunes for a few weeks, and I was able to see that some songs worked better than others. I found that "Stayin' Alive" by the Bee Gees is a great first song.

After the students get used to playing steady beats with music, they can begin to use different combinations to reflect changes in the music. For example, in "Jump in the Line" by Harry Belafonte the chorus has a four-feel and the verse has a two-feel. If you don't know what that means right now, it's okay, just listen to the song and you'll get it. With the song turned off, I can demonstrate four beats, then two beats, and explain how one thing is half of the other. We can work on that together for a while, then turn on the song again.

When we get to that section, I say "half" and we play the two-feel. After listening to that part of the song a few times and working on the comparison of two and four away from the music a few times, the students can play the beats just like the recording. They're able to learn the concept of dividing something in half by learning how to change from a four-feel to a two-feel in the song. This concept is also found in many content standards and/or learning goals from subjects other than music.

The song "Jump in the Line" was in a movie called Beetlejuice *that several of my students really liked. Although it wasn't a hit song at the time, the popularity of the movie with the kids made the song a good choice. I always try to choose songs that would be relevant to them when possible.*

This same concept applies to doubling the beat as well. In a song like "Gangnam Style" by Psy, there is a section that builds intensity and doubles the beat, then doubles it again. When we play songs like that, I say "double" when we get to that section, and we play eight strokes instead of four, then move to sixteen if needed, but that usually just turns out to be a roll. We work on it away from the song first, learning the relationship of doubling four beats to get eight strokes.

If you don't know the song, give it a listen and you'll hear the build. Songs that have some type of double in them are quite common. "Gangnam Style" also has some cool moves that can easily be added for great effects. All you need to do is watch the video. Although it's an older song, it has stayed a part of popular culture, appearing on TV, in movies, and in video games.

As mentioned earlier, clapping is also a great way to add variety to your songs and can be quite effective with songs where less is happening musically. It can be a great way to break up a tune and define different verses, choruses, or other elements of music. For example, in "Jump in the Line," there's a section that has four stomps representing a dance. Students can clap in this section and it adds a nice variation to the song. Clapping can also be part of the main beat of the song. The perfect example is "We Will Rock You" by Queen. Students can play two tones and clap once and have great success very quickly. This is another example of a great first song.

Combining different tones to make patterns will make things much more interesting, and also allow students to work on more complicated music. For example, a tune like "Day-O" by Harry Belafonte, another song from the movie *Beetlejuice*, can be played with two bass tones and one open tone. Combinations can be as simple or as complicated as you like. It's also possible to start with a straight beat, then add a combination when students are ready. Students might add hand gestures and movements that can become part of the performance. Sometimes movements can be added that are based on popular dances that go with the song.

In "Stayin' Alive," there is a hand movement John Travolta makes in the movie where he points his finger in the air and moves it up and down across his body. If you're unfamiliar with that move, look it up and you'll see it. It's simple, it can be done while seated, and it's great fun for both the performers

Paraprofessional Chris Miles and Teacher John Finch were great helpers with my middle school drummers!

and the audience alike. Plus, it's historically accurate. You're teaching music history and popular culture.

The teachers and classroom aides might have ideas, too. Sometimes sign language can be worked into a routine with the music. Other movements can reflect song lyrics, and we've even used handmade projects to enhance our performances. There's no limit or standard; it's all up to you. Watching the songs evolve can be a lot of fun.

When choosing songs, try to find something that will work for everyone, but don't lose sleep over it if things don't go as planned. Song choice can be very personal. We all have different reasons for choosing certain music. If after working for a few sessions you feel like you made a bad choice, that's okay. You can always try something else, but keep in mind that your first instinct might not be a bad choice. Everyone isn't going to react the same to all the songs you choose. You might find people that don't seem to be participating or maybe they're reluctant to play. That might just be the way they operate. Maybe a student doesn't do anything with his or her hands, but he or she can feel the vibrations of the music and rock back and forth in his or her seat. For some students, just listening to music makes them happy. The level of participation for each student is different, but the experience of playing along with recorded music can be one of the best things that happen to your students during their time at school.

AUDIO EQUIPMENT	SONGS
PA System	"Stayin' Alive" by the Bee Gees
Subwoofer	"Jump in the Line" by Harry Belafonte
	"Day-O" by Harry Belafonte
MOVIE	"Gangnum Style" by Psy
	"We Will Rock You" by Queen
Beetlejuice by Tim Burton	

INCORPORATING OTHER INSTRUMENTS

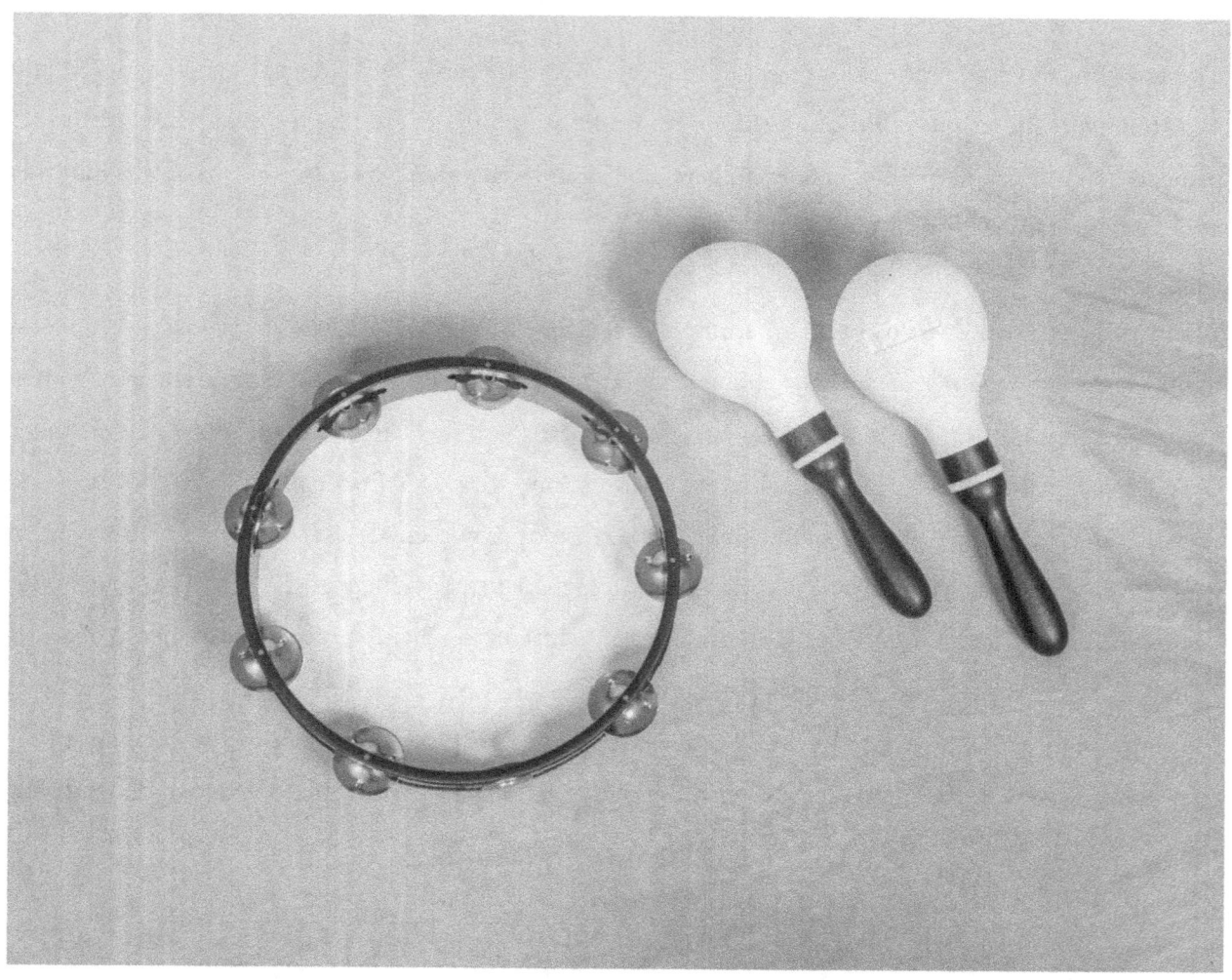

After working on several different songs with our drummers, I found that certain tunes had a speed or "tempo" that seemed too fast and somehow felt uncomfortable. What I started to think was that some tunes just didn't work. One day, the band students and I were working on music for the middle school spring band concert. One of those tunes had a maraca part, so I was working on it with a student during class. I put the maracas on the stand by my stereo after our class was finished.

Later, the hand drummers came in for our weekly meeting, and we were using a CD for our next lesson. I knew there were two songs on the CD that I wanted to use, but I didn't know the song order, so I had to check each one. While scanning the tracks on the CD, I landed on the wrong one and it was a song that was too fast. Just as I was moving to press the NEXT button, I saw my maracas sitting on the stand and heard maracas in the song. It just so happened I had an extra set in the percussion cabinet, so I tried showing one of my hand drummers how to play them and it worked. She liked it and was able to play it correctly fairly quickly. By accident, I found a new way to teach. If a tune is a little too fast, sometimes you can use maracas to play rhythms. I decided we needed to find some maracas for the group.

USING MARACAS

We try to avoid holding them like a club or baseball bat. We hold our maracas just like a drumstick, with the thumb across from the first finger. We never put the thumb on the outside. It helps control the maraca and makes the students think more about the technique they're using when the thumb is across from the first finger.

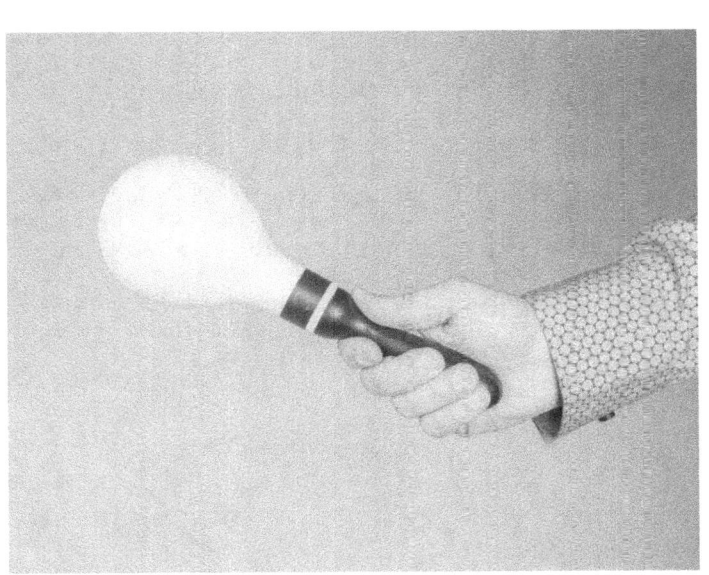

If not all students can hold the maracas properly, it will still be okay, just make accommodations when needed. Some of my students could only use one hand, and others needed someone to move their hands for them. You can always make something work. With everything I do, we can always modify our process to include someone with different abilities.

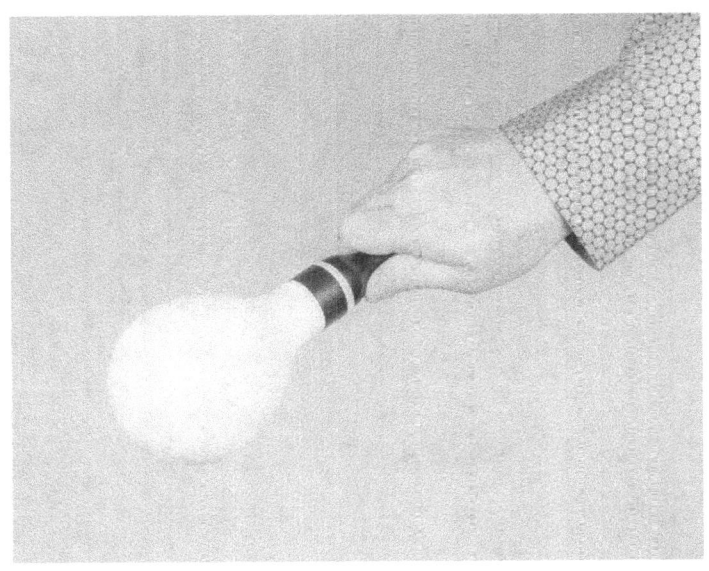

I use three basic maraca techniques with my students: alternating strokes, hands together, and clicking the handles.

Alternating Strokes

This is the most common technique and can be used all the time. This is done repeatedly and usually on each beat. Start with the maracas right in front of you. RIGHT SHAKE, LEFT SHAKE, RIGHT SHAKE, LEFT SHAKE on each beat. I like to think of playing strokes with the maracas like hitting a pretend drum in the air. If you think of it that way, it helps you understand there is an end to the stroke. You don't want the maraca to hit your legs and you don't want it moving all the way up over your shoulders. You just want a simple stroke a couple of inches high. The concept that you have to stop the maraca is much clearer when thinking of the "air drum."

Hands Together

These strokes can be used more visually by moving the maracas around, such as to the left, then to the right. You simply shake the maracas at the same time. This can be done on every other beat, or during long or slow parts of songs. If you're listening to the drummer in the music, it can be on the backbeat like a snare

drum playing on counts two and four. If you have no idea what that means, it's okay, don't worry about it. I have a lesson about the backbeat on my YouTube channel @*LearnWithDrums* if you are interested in learning more.

Clicking the Handles

By flipping the handles towards the inside, the player has a simple way to create variation in sound. The clicking sound comes from the handles striking each other instead of the beads shaking inside. A variety of rhythms can be used. This is our most complex technique, but very effective if you need to add more variation to your playing.

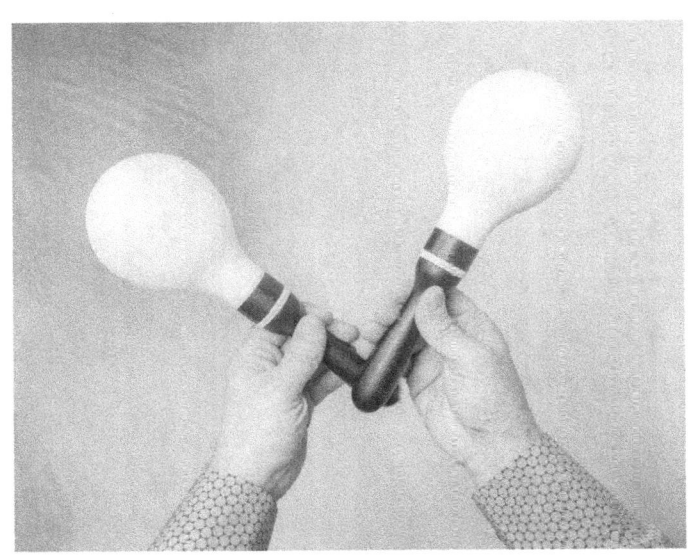

When using the different techniques of the maracas, there can be many more visual elements than when playing a drum. They're usually made of bright colors which quickly catch the eyes. Keep that in mind when planning a performance and use it to your advantage. You can have everyone shake to the left, then shake to the right. You can make fun movements to go along with the music that can even reflect the lyrics.

Usually in the beginning, just getting students to hold the maracas can be the goal. After that, getting them on the beat should be the next goal. The last thing to focus on would be working to have all the maracas move in the same direction. When trying to get everyone's hands in the same place on the same strokes, be sure (if you're facing the students) to play your rhythms with backwards hands so the "left and right" are correct for them, not you. When facing the class, you should always think of your movements as if you are looking in a mirror.

When I need the students to stop shaking the maracas, I tell them, "Sticks in your pits." Everyone puts the bulb end of the maraca towards their armpit. I also do this in my concert bands with my drummers when they are noodling and tapping with their sticks.

For a fun holiday lesson using maracas, check out my YouTube channel **@LearnWithDrums**

USING TAMBOURINES

We also discovered that tambourines can be used for a different effect in our performances. After the success with the maracas, when we heard a tambourine in a song, we thought we should give it a try and it worked. I started reaching out for funding to buy tambourines. Once I had enough for everyone, we tried it as a class.

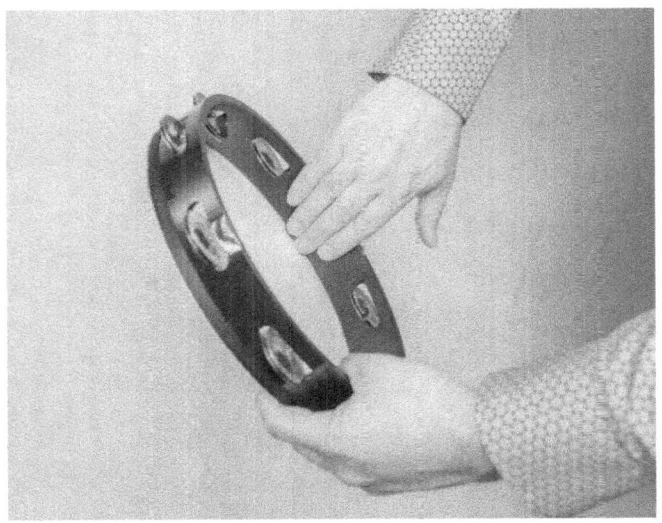

Playing Position

The key to successfully using the tambourine is holding it properly. The thumb needs to go on top of the head, then the fingers close around the shell. Most tambourines have a hole in the shell where there are no jingles. As mentioned before, the hole is there to mount the tambourine on a cymbal stand if you were playing in a band or orchestra. That's also the best place to hold it with your hand. Be sure to tell your students they don't need to stick their fingers in the hole.

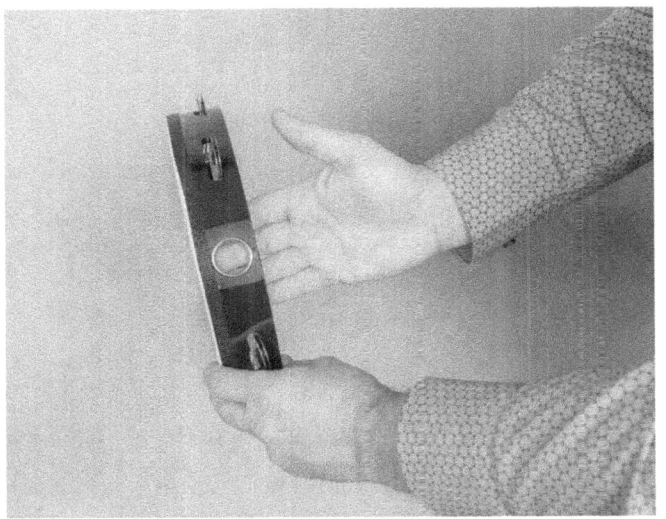

The Basic Stroke

While holding the tambourine in a vertical position, move your wrist like you're holding a garden hose and watering the lawn. Strike the head of the tambourine in the center with your opposite hand. Think of moving the tambourine "into" your other hand. The

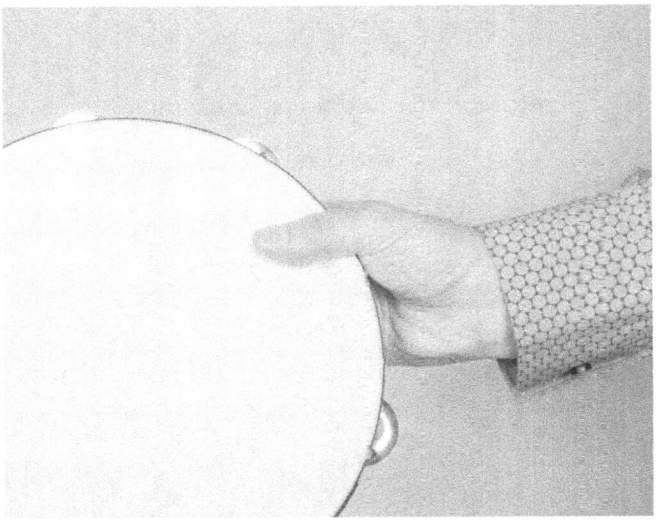

combination of those two moves is the basic stroke we all picture in our minds when we think of someone playing a tambourine. Try and use your wrists in addition to your arms. If you just move your arms, you might look like a wind-up toy.

The Shake Roll

Think of twisting your hand as if you were turning a doorknob. The faster you twist, the more sound you get. Try it for short and long periods. Just like the maracas, the tambourine is a very visual instrument. You can shake it in different directions for fun effects.

When you need to be quiet, you can hold the tambourine diagonally so the jingles won't rattle. The best way to stop the sound with the tambourine is to put it down. It's very hard to keep it from making noise when you're holding it. I have my students put it on their drum with the head side down when I need them to be quiet for instruction.

When buying tambourines, there are dozens of choices from dozens of companies. Be sure to get a ten-inch instrument with a synthetic head. It makes it much easier for the students to have a larger target to hit. When using a tambourine without a head, it's more difficult to play. I also like to use tambourines with only a single row of jingles. Remember, less volume is best for our situation.

If you decide to use additional instruments such as maracas or tambourines, you have to figure out where to put them when you aren't using them. I store my maracas in a large case with wheels made to hold percussion instruments called a "trap case." (It's called that because it's able to hold many of the drummer's different contraptions.) It's handy because I can roll the case to each student and have them take a pair of maracas, then move it out of the way. When we're finished, I can roll the case to each student and have them put the maracas back in the case, then roll the case away.

There was a time when I had a trap case that had a tray in the top. I would put the maracas in the bottom and the tambourines in the top tray. It worked great for that situation with a smaller group. At one point, I had a closet that had shelves where I kept the tambourines. When we used them, I had each kid come and get one, then each kid put his or hers away. I stood at the closet, had the students line up, and I helped them handle the tambourines.

After the students learned the routine, I started having them take tambourines to the staff members and any students that might not be able to get their own. As the students got a little older, some were able to get more than two and pass them out. I've had all different storage setups, from cardboard boxes to drum cases. They will all do the job, it just depends on your budget and what works for you. Make sure you put them away somewhere because instruments that are left out WILL be picked up and played!

If we were having a performance or I could have everything set up before the class, I put the tambourines under the seats, head down, with maracas inside of the tambourine.

I found it's important when I first get out the hand percussion instruments to let the students start shaking them right away. It's hard to resist shaking and hitting, so it's important to just let them go for it as soon as possible. I have the students shake their

instruments as fast as they can as I give instructions and play with them. For example, "Up high, down low, out front, now shake it slow." Usually, we can shake the silliness out of our system and then learn some rhythms. If you lose control of the class, just say, "Shake it out!" and shake your instrument high and low, left and right until they all join in with you, and then you'll be able to get their attention. Once you're done with the lesson or song, you can have students put their instruments under their chairs. Remember, instruments under chairs can't make any sounds!

Performing with percussion instruments like maracas and tambourines uses different muscles and motions than playing a conga drum. This can be beneficial to developing coordination and motor skills but might present new challenges. When I first started teaching my hand drum groups, I didn't use anything *but* the drums. With some groups, I wait until they have a really strong understanding of the drum before I pass out maracas. It will be different for everyone.

When you try something new, it's important to be patient. If everyone is not even close to looking the same way while playing the tambourine or not even holding it right, it doesn't mean it won't happen over time. By the end of the year, it will be better. Always remember the most challenging time for the teacher is when *everyone* is new, but that's also the best time because you can't go wrong. There are no expectations; you're simply sharing something fun!

PART 6: CLASSES

WHAT DOES A CLASS LOOK LIKE?

Now let's say you have some drums. You've figured out how to store them and how to set them up with the other items in the room. You've figured out some basic techniques, and most importantly, you have kids to teach. Now how do you start?

At this point, you've read about what I do with students and how I developed my method. I've also mentioned I have some videos on YouTube. There's more information on my website, SpecialNeedforMusic.com, too. The one thing we haven't discussed yet is what happens in a real class. Let's look at a sample from my former high school.

About This Class

This high school class meets for fifty minutes and includes students in grades 9-12, starting in the first week of February. This group will have a concert during the school day in the band room in May. Today, there will be six students. In this particular group, many students need a great deal of assistance. In addition to myself, the classroom teacher and three aides are here to help. This class varies from year to year as to the number of students, their learning strengths, and their physical abilities.

Four students have taken this class with me in middle school and the other two are new to drumming this year. Two of the aides and the classroom teacher have been with me for many years, and one aide is new to drumming this year. All are coming from the MH Classroom for one day each week. They have all attended classes before and we are not learning any new material today, but we have not had classes in several weeks due to snow days, vacations, and illness.

Preparation Before Class

Chairs are set up in an arc with name tags on the seats. The drums are in the room but a few feet away from the chairs. The audio system is ready and songs are on a playlist. I have a large folder I keep in the closet with the drums containing nametags, a legal pad, and a pen. On the legal pad is a list of what we did last time and a seating chart. There is a list of songs and my lesson plan. This group has not worked with maracas or tambourines yet this year because they don't seem like the right fit with their abilities.

Five Minutes: Set-Up

Students enter and take their seats holding their name tags. I then move a drum in front of each student and they put their nametag in front of their drum on the floor.

Five Minutes: FUN-damentals

I try to use demonstration with little verbal instruction. I say, "Fingers together, thumb out of the way." I hold my hand up showing my fingers together and thumb out. Then I play open tones, demonstrating fingers on the edge of the drum. The class joins in. Random beats become a steady beat with the staff members, then the students begin to follow. We switch hands a few times. Next, I demonstrate bass tones then we begin playing the bass tones as a group. Random strokes again quickly evolve to a steady beat, then an eight-count exercise. I stop and ask, "What's it called when we go back and forth?"

Students then answer "alternate" and we begin alternating hands with bass tones and open tones. This evolves into an exercise of eight beats of bass tones and eight beats of open tones. We practice this for a while, then we switch to a combination of four bass tones and four open tones. I don't give verbal instructions, I just demonstrate. At this point, the students all know the fundamentals and the exercises move fairly quickly.

Eight Minutes: Roll

As we play our open tones and bass tones, I ask the class what it's called when we alternate our hands quickly. Someone answers with "the roll," demonstrating while they answer! I start to play a soft roll and the class joins in. I play a little louder and the class does the same, then I get softer. We practice a few times, then I abruptly yell "stop!" We all freeze, then I yell, "Go!" and we all start again. They love the stop-and-go type of roll. It's like playing peek-a-boo, but with drums! In this group, I've figured out that doing the wave is not a successful exercise, but using soft-and-loud and stop-and-go rolls works very well.

Seven Minutes: I Play, You Play

The students' names and favorite foods are listed on my seating chart. I go around to each student and I play and say each example, then the students also lead with their own choice. For example, "Mikey likes pi-zza", then Mikey will lead from his seat. I'm always sure to have each student try it twice. When they make mistakes, we all still play it back the right way. If the mistake happens again the second time, we can break it down and just do one word at a time.

Seven Minutes: Song Number One, "Stayin' Alive" by The Bee Gees

We review the move that we make with this song where we point one finger up and away from our body, then move across and down in front of our body, just like John Travolta does in the movie. It's a simple move we can make from our seats. We also talk about how we will practice open tones and clapping. After this review, I turn on the song and we play along. It's almost a five-minute song and very repetitive, so it's a great song to start with. We're getting a chance to develop a steady beat, moving and clapping on the chorus, and using open tones for the verses. Since it's a long song and review, we only run through it once.

Mistakes are made and we correct them as we go without stopping. The aides are helping students. Some have to move hands for students at times. When they're not helping move hands or correcting, they play. At this point in the year, the aides know that you can't keep correcting too much; the students need to try on their own. Corrections are only about hands moving the right way. Sometimes the steady beat isn't there yet, but the students are following the teacher and aides as best they can.

Three Minutes: Song Number Two, "We Will Rock You" by Queen.

We review the rhythms found in the song first. In this song, we will be playing open, open, clap. I demonstrate very slowly. They imitate. We make sure everyone is clapping correctly. We practice the beat slowly at first. We then start the recording and play along. Since this is a song we've performed before, I shouldn't need to stop, so we try a complete run-through. It's only a two-minute song, so we could do it again if we feel it's necessary.

The song is a good choice for this particular group because some of these students have difficulties with quickly combining the two different concepts of striking the drum and clapping. This song helps them learn. I'm careful to make sure students don't get too frustrated while playing. If they're having trouble with a section of the music and get too frustrated, we move on. There is a history of behavior challenges with this group, so we keep a safe balance of learning and playing. This is another time when we can't correct too much. There has to be time for students to work things out on their own.

Ten Minutes: Song Number Three, "YMCA" by The Village People

We start by reviewing the moves. We use our arms to make a "Y", then we work on the "M". We find that the M is a little different than we thought, and we try to correct the arms to make it better than last time. The "C" is easy but we talk about how it has to be positioned so the audience can read it. Some students are doing it the wrong way. We make it better than last time. We check the "A" and it's good, so we make all four moves very slowly a few times and we say the letters as we do the moves. We also clap three times after we make the letters, so we keep our place in the music. We review the entire sequence together slowly before we play with the music. Then we play the recording. We clap on the introduction, then begin open tones. We use the extended version of this song, so we run through and correct problems as we go without stopping the song.

Five Minutes: Cleanup

This group is now to the point where I have a student collect the name tags, keeping them in order for the next time. I store them in my lesson folder. Then I have each student bring his or her drum to the storage closet and I stack it. After each student brings his or her drum to me, I ask them to get the drums from the staff members and bring them to me at the storage closet door. After everything is put away, the students line up at the door with the aides and we say goodbye for the week. I make sure to note what we covered and what we should do next time. I have very short and simple notes on my legal pad. When the kids leave, I put my folder away in the closet with the drums and I'm off to the middle school.

This is just a sample of one of my classes and if I taught this same class again, I'm sure the timing would be different. The times don't matter as much as following the order. If you work in this order, students progress with the building complexity throughout the lesson. Some students might be able to add more actions quickly, and others might leave a few things out for the more complicated songs. That's okay, they can add movements or rhythms at their own pace.

Once it is finally time to play, we must be sure to prepare BEFORE we get together with the students. Always make sure to practice your material in advance. It doesn't take much time; you just need to be familiar with the things you're going to present to the students. You may even discover that you end up really liking hand drums and might even want to study more outside of this program. That's great!

PART 7: PERFORMANCE

PUTTING IT ALL TOGETHER

The difference between my method and other music programs for individuals with special needs is the performance. I treat my drum groups the same as my school bands. We learn skills and we apply them to music. After several lessons, we perform music that showcases our talents.

My school groups always performed in the band room at first with a small audience of family members. We had an area in the room we considered the "stage" where we had the instruments set up, and an area we considered the "audience" where we had chairs for special guests. As you and your students get more comfortable performing, you can invite more people to watch and increase the complexity of your show. In addition to the classroom, we also performed in an auditorium and a school gymnasium. One group even traveled to an elementary school. We went "on tour" and we talked about what a concert tour is for professional musicians and entertainers.

At first, our performances consisted of simply playing a few songs in the classroom for our guests. This is a great accomplishment for the students, and if we stopped there, we had a great educational experience. Over the last several years, our performances have evolved to include projects from outside the music class. In the next few pages, I will share with you some of the things we have come up with over the years, but it's important to remember that you don't need to design anything fancy. You might not get to the point where you're ready to add anything "extra" to your concerts at first, but just like my groups, more can be added over time.

Here are a few "extra" lessons and topics we have explored over the last several years that go past performing music. You can enhance your performance based on the strengths of the people and resources available to you. This is a great opportunity to include other classes and disciplines and truly be cross-curricular. But remember, there is nothing wrong with just inviting parents to watch their kids play tunes during the school day. That's still good, too!

Unit Concept
The performance can be a great vehicle for relating several different concepts into one cohesive educational "unit." The kids love having a concert, and what a better way to teach kids than by using something they love?

In the early stages of my first middle school drum group, the special education teacher and I would talk each week about how we could prepare for our concert. What we didn't realize at the time is we were creating a unit. She had ideas that I didn't even consider. Her point of view was completely different than mine. By working together, we came up with great activities that allowed the kids to show their efforts. It's so important to work with the strengths of your helpers. Things might not be the same each time if you have new staff members, and that's okay. You'll find your activities can change to suit the abilities of your group. That goes for students and staff. For example, one year we were able to do a line dance because one of our paraprofessionals had experience with that type of dance.

The concept of planning an event gives students plenty of opportunities to work on life skills with their classroom teacher outside of their time learning music with me. The kids can create invitations and figure out how many people will be coming to the concert. They can bake cookies or make food when appropriate, figuring out how many treats to prepare based on how many people would be coming to the show. Students can make posters to hang in the school advertising their event. They can make decorations to hang in the performance room for the concert and signs for their drums. We usually have large colorful nametags on the drums for each student. Sometimes all of those things can be related to each other visually or have a common theme.

There was a time when I worked with a teacher who always wanted themed shows. Although we weren't always able to, sometimes choosing a theme that pulled all the songs together made for exciting and fun preparations. We had a Caribbean show where everyone wore tropical shirts and the students made a palm tree. One year we hosted Game Night, and everyone wore sports jerseys. Each student could pick a favorite sport and make a list of fun facts or choose an athlete and find information about him or her. When we performed theme shows, all our songs were somehow related.

This is Lauren Cox and Nanette Cox. Ms. Cox was the middle school teacher I worked with in the very beginning. She always had great ideas for our students.

Sharing and Cross-Curricular Projects

When we see the word "share" in modern times, we immediately think of social media, but it can be old-school paper invitations or posters, too. It's important for the students to invite others. Each of my past groups has made invitations for their teachers and principals inviting them to the concerts.

At my last school, the students created invitations to send to their former teachers as well. At one point, special education classes from the elementary school came to see the middle school concert. Sharing successful performances on social media can be fun, too, if you have permission.

I always like to record the concert to share with the students when possible. Back in the old days, I used to set up a video camera in the corner and let it record the show. The performers love to see themselves, and it's a great way for their families and loved ones to remember the special event. That was back before everyone had a camera on their phone and we had to use videotape! Of course, technology has evolved and students can make recordings of events much easier now.

One time we made a movie for the students using video editing software to include clips from our performances and pictures taken throughout the year. This would be an outstanding project for a video production class. Students studying photography could be involved in taking pictures and videos. Maybe there's a yearbook club that could work with you, too. It's always a good idea to make arrangements for a friend or parent to take pictures so you can remember and celebrate the event if student helpers aren't available. Sometimes we were able to incorporate the high school technology students by having them record the event and use video streaming to broadcast the performance live on the school's website. People could see the concert without being there. My wife was able to watch our show from home. Back in the old days, that was a big deal!

Not all of the extras involved technology. Some concerts incorporated projects that the kids made in their art class. For example, there was a year when we performed a song by the rock band KISS at the middle school. The kids worked with the art teacher to make masks of the KISS makeup. The art teacher was excited to be part of the event. That year we were even featured on the KISS website. Everyone was thrilled!

When we performed the song, "Royals" by Lorde, the students made crowns. They went to a restaurant that was known for being the king of burgers and asked if they could have some paper crowns. They used glitter and construction paper to make great additions to each student's crown, making a great look for the performance.

This is Logan Wise, Lauren Cox, and high school teacher Nicole Sankey. Miss Sankey did great work with our students.

We can also relate our music to pop culture. If we're playing a Bee Gees tune, we could check out what was happening in history in the 1970s when disco became popular, and learn why *Saturday Night Fever* was such a successful movie. Students of all ages and abilities can relate music to historical events and people. These activities can be for the student performers or student leaders as an enrichment project.

Decorations

Over the years, my students have made all kinds of decorations to hang in the classroom for performances. Sometimes they involved the art teacher, but usually, they were simple activities they would work on with their teachers and classroom aides. Sometimes there were posters and even banners made from large bulletin board paper that featured pictures and artwork as well as information about the music we were playing. For example, when we had a theme called "Rock the Decades," we presented information about the musicians from each era, as well as facts about 70s disco, 80s pop, and more!

Student Leaders

Our drummers have also worked with other student groups to make decorations and projects together. Working with student leadership groups or honors students can strengthen communication skills on both sides. Developing social skills is always a welcomed activity, and it makes everyone feel good. Many schools are looking to incorporate student leadership into their programs, and this provided the perfect opportunity.

When I used a couple of my band students as class helpers, they learned how to interact, how to help set up the room, and how to help certain individuals. One year I had a student leader that created a fun maraca routine that went along with the lyrics of a popular tune of the day. We ended up using the movements in our performance and it became a crowd favorite!

In the early days, I would have my band kids come to see the drummers as a way to practice performing in front of an audience. They were super supportive, both verbally and through their actions. At the first concert, there were messages of encouragement and praise written all over the marker board. The drummers felt like celebrities! It's amazing what student leaders can do for students with special needs.

Setting

Back when we began, having a concert during the school day was the best way for us to perform. We started small, having the kids set up in the band room and inviting their parents and

> One thing to consider when planning where to perform is the transportation of your gear. Make sure you can move it because sometimes your students will not be able to help move heavy equipment.

loved ones to watch. By starting in the classroom, there were fewer distractions and it reduced interruptions in everyone's daily routine. I like to think of it as a classroom with a window. I showed our guests what we do in class every week. It allowed an up-close and personal experience where the audience could see the kids' faces. Some years that was the only performance we held, and it was great. The experience is always an emotional and meaningful event.

Recently, performances are less like a class and more like a traditional concert. The audience has grown, and students have been invited to play at an elementary school, an art festival, and even a school assembly. In most school districts, everyone will be kind to the students with special needs.

The administrators, school board members, and the community will most likely be very supportive of the group, so be sure to invite them to your concerts, too.

I did discover that even though audiences are supportive, sometimes if the crowd is too large, too loud, or in a giant room, the performance can be difficult. Students can be easily distracted and overwhelmed. For example, a high school pep rally in a gymnasium is not a good place for a performance. Even performing for a quiet audience on a large stage with bright lights can be a challenge. On the other hand, I had great success when I took a middle school drum group to play for elementary kids. They performed on a small stage in a cafeteria and all of the kids in the audience sat on the floor. There were no spotlights, just the

High school paraprofessionals Angela Rotella, Carol Nealey, and Marla Miskimen worked hard to help students with their drumming class and prepare for special events.

regular room lights. It was also fun for students to see their former teachers in the audience! Most recently, I've had a high school group perform at an art festival as part of a larger program where there were other performances. With the help of some dedicated adults, we had a great show. They were rock stars that day!

By having the concert during the day, we avoided some potential pitfalls, the first of which is bussing. Many students depend on the bus for getting to and from school, so coming back to school for an evening concert is sometimes difficult. Also, having classroom aids after school could be a problem with union contracts. Hosting the concert as part of a regular school day was our best choice.

Publicity

Parent involvement is typically encouraged in education. Hosting a concert is a great way to get people into your school or organization. You can advertise the concert as much as you like. This can be as simple as making signs to hang at the school, and it can go as far as writing a press release for the local newspaper, contacting a radio station, or even recording a video commercial. Video commercials could be played on the school announcements, posted on the school website, or shared on social media. Some schools might have production classes that could work together with the performing musicians. I've had a group of students that worked on a live stream of one of our concerts. Projects like this are great lessons for both the performers and other students.

Contact your local newspaper and share information with them when good things are happening. Make contact at least a week before the event so an article has time to be published. Sometimes a reporter will stop by for a visit. Don't take it personally if nobody shows up. My groups have been skipped over many times, but they were also on the front page a few times, too. Everyone loves to see themselves in the paper. If your students appear in the newspaper, be sure to get a couple of extra copies that day and hang one up for everyone to see. Keep things fun. Whatever you decide to do with publicity has to be within your comfort zone.

Program

Some performance groups like to have a printed program to hand out at their performance. It typically contains information about the performance, such as a list of songs, student names, upcoming events, and even fundraiser information. Pictures, drawings, fun facts, and trivia questions can all be excellent additions. If you have students work on the programs, you have an opportunity to teach a variety of skills at whatever level you choose.

Reception

The concept of the reception can easily relate to several different life skills and lessons in a variety of subjects. My middle school groups sometimes made cookies to share with guests after the performance. At the high school that wasn't an option, but sometimes someone would donate pizza and treats for the students as a celebration of their hard work. When student leaders worked with the drum class throughout the year, they joined the party, too. Things varied from year to year based on the building schedule, but when we could work with other student organizations, things always seemed better.

Most recently, I've started working with a vocational program for adults with special needs. At their concert, they presented examples from their food class at their reception. They had a variety of snacks prepared by the individuals in the group, and they used the time after the concert to share tasty treats and have an open house to show the different projects they work on throughout the week. Not only were staff members able to share their musical success with families, but their daily work as well.

This is Christy Bennett, Christina Fowler, Nancy Hunter, Kim Domer, Angelica Mendoza, and Luke Bordner. They are staff members at Advocates for Success. They help drummers play their instruments and incorporate other elements such as their food class and art projects into their performances.

Certified Occupational Therapy Assistant Farrah Raines nominated me for an award for educators that support students with special needs. She was also the one who encouraged me to present at my first professional conference.

Closing

There are so many great learning opportunities when hosting a concert. The unique thing about the concert, compared to typical academic assessments, is that the students use every single skill they've learned all at the same time. There's only one chance to make it work and everyone gets to see it! But remember to have realistic expectations. Mistakes happen, things won't go as planned, and there will be distractions. It's okay, you're already making a difference just by simply trying.

Think about all of the questions someone who has never seen a concert could ask. Every question is an opportunity to learn. Just start with an open mind and the concert can be a fantastic learning experience for many. Remember to start with simple ideas and add more concepts as you and your students become more comfortable and confident. I started with only one kid. You can, too!

Stay in touch at SpecialNeedforMusic.com and share your experiences!

CONCLUSION

When I started this program, I had no idea I would ever be sharing a teaching method with other professionals. I wasn't trying to write a book, make presentations at conferences, or create instructional videos. I was just trying to teach music to a child who was left out.

At first, I didn't feel comfortable inviting a bunch of people to see what we were doing in my class. That was way outside of my comfort zone. But eventually, I decided to host a concert with just a few parents to see how it would work. What I learned from that first performance is that parents just want to see their kids find success, whatever that may look like. I learned that success looks different for everyone, and it was super different than what I was trained to look for as a band director. Once I realized that teaching music to students with special needs was about MORE than just playing the right notes, and it was certainly NOT about reading fancy sheet music, I was able to reach my students, both young and old, in ways I never could have done before.

From then on, at each concert, we seemed to be able to invite a few more people, play a couple more beats, and add some cool new moves. It has evolved over time to include more people, both young and old, that were otherwise left out of the fantastic experience of not only making music but PERFORMING music in front of a real audience. Hopefully, now you can help someone else fill the special need for music in their life!

Good luck and happy drumming!

SPECIAL THANKS TO THE CONTRIBUTORS TO THIS BOOK

Sarah Dursik

Win Dozer

Christy Howell

Jim Howell, Jr.

Kris Howell

Dave Huthmacher

Tyler King

Jessica Klingler

Linda Ligman

Farrah Raines

Mikey Rogers

Walt Shade

Chad Shumaker

ABOUT THE AUTHOR

Mr. Howell began his teaching career in 1998. He is currently the band director and music teacher at Osnaburg Local Schools in East Canton, Ohio, and formerly taught band and music at Claymont City Schools in Uhrichsville, Ohio.

Since 2009, Mr. Howell has developed a teaching method that includes a performance group for students with special needs at both the middle school and high school levels. These groups provide opportunities to students that did not have a chance to participate in a musical performance in the past and have evolved into a great source of pride for the students and their parents.

Mr. Howell and his students have been featured in the documentary film, "922 From Academic Watch to Academic Wow!" and they have been featured several times in the Times Reporter Ohio newspaper. Mr. Howell has presented his teaching methods at professional conferences for both special education and music educators such as:

- Texas Autism Conference
- Milestones National Autism Conference
- OCALI (Ohio Center for Autism and Low Incidence) Conference
- Ohio Music Education Association Conference

In addition to his work as a school music teacher, Mr. Howell has also created a performing group at Advocates for Success, an organization that provides life skills training and vocational programs for adults with disabilities in New Philadelphia, Ohio.

Mr. Howell holds a Master's degree in Educational Administration from Ashland University and a Bachelor's degree in Music Education from Bowling Green State University.